THE
ROYAL CHEF
AT HOME

bright sky press
HOUSTON, TEXAS

2365 Rice Blvd., Suite 202
Houston, Texas 77005

ISBN: 978-1-942945-52-9

10 9 8 7 6 5 4 3 2

Library of Congress Cataloging-in-Publication Data on file with the publisher.

Editorial Director: Lauren Gow
Designer: Marla Y. Garcia
Writer: Susan Ruffins

Printed by Bookmasters

THE ROYAL CHEF

AT HOME

Easy Seasonal Entertaining

DARREN McGRADY
Photography by DICK PATRICK

bright sky press

HOUSTON, TEXAS

TABLE OF
CONTENTS

ACKNOWLEDGEMENTS

"The joys of the table belong equally to all ages, conditions and times:
they mix with all other pleasures and remain
the last to console us for their loss."

– Brillat-Savarin –

I've cooked in some of the grandest palaces in the world for kings, queens, presidents and celebrities—too many to mention. Yet, the biggest pleasure of all is cooking at home for family and friends. For them, I want each dish to be a perfect expression of gratitude for everything they bring to my life.

I couldn't have written this book or *Eating Royally* without the love and support of my wife Wendy, who makes it all worthwhile, and of my children, Kelly, Lexie and Harry, whose companionship I treasure inside and outside of the kitchen. I love you four with all my heart.

Thanks to my mother Pauline and my nan Florrie Lambert, who through innumerable home cooked meals broadened my palate and showed me the depths of their love. My deepest respect and love to my dad Michael, for supporting us all and providing a stable home for my brother Chris, my sister Sacha and me.

Thank you to my writer and good friend Susan Ruffins for working with me on my second book and translating my stream of consciousness into something sane and worth reading. Her discipline kept us on track and moving forward.

Thank you to Dick Patrick for his amazing photography throughout this book, bringing my food to life, and thanks also to his assistant Jesse "The Hands" Chacon and to Rocio Gonzales for all her help setting up shots. A thank you to Carmaleta Whiteley for making our tea shots memorable and for her perfect pouring.

Thanks to my agent Laura Cutler Herbert for nudging me every day to get the book done. You are the best agent in the world. Thanks to Donnie and Martha Miller, Dee Wyly and especially to Debbie, John and Kacy Tolleson (you know why!).

Thank you to Colin Snider at Bentwood of Dallas for letting me use his gorgeous kitchen for my cover shot and to Stephan Kjeldgard for jumping in when I needed a butler to hold canapés. A special thank you to David Rodriguez for the fabulous lemons photo.

And finally, thank you to Fiona Bills and Lauren Gow at Bright Sky Press for helping me create the book I really wanted to share with you. I hope you enjoy it!

– Darren McGrady

A project like this takes an enormous amount of time, coordination, dedication and team work. I would like to say thank you to my team mates for helping bring this project to fruition. To Darren and Susan for believing that I had the vision to bring these recipes to life in photographs. To Jesse Chacon for being a steady and loyal assistant. And finally to my wife Stacey and my daughters Sydney and Lea for allowing me to use some of our precious family time to work on this project. I hope the pictures make you all proud.

– Dick Patrick

Many thanks to the people at Bright Sky Press, especially Fiona Bills and Lauren Gow who patiently guided us through the process from start to finish. Their talented advice helped immeasurably, especially in those manuscript moments where the forest is difficult to see for all the trees. I want to thank the ever patient and generous Dick Patrick, whose lovely photos grace the pages of this book. My deepest regards and thanks go to Darren McGrady, without whose friendship and enthusiasm this book would never have happened. Things really are more fun the second time around!

My greatest appreciation though is for the support and encouragement given unstintingly by my husband and children. Seth, Theo and Olivia, you make everything seem possible.

– Susan Ruffins

INTRODUCTION

*"When we no longer have good cooking in the world,
we will have no literature, nor high and sharp intelligence,
nor friendly gatherings, nor social harmony."*

– Marie-Antoine Carême –

There are two things I know: To eat well, you must know how to cook. To live well, you must share your life with others. Now, I don't profess these maxims to be universally true. They are however true for me. The years I spent working in the kitchens of Buckingham Palace, Windsor and Balmoral Castles cooking for the British royal family taught me the fundamentals of cuisine and trained me as a chef. But being a chef is my job; being a cook is who I am. For me it is about beauty, nourishment, friendship and love. While I like to cook for myself, it's sharing food with family and friends that brings me the greatest satisfaction.

My first book, *Eating Royally: Recipes and Remembrances from a Palace Kitchen*, was about my experiences as a chef immersed in a world that is almost unrecognizable today. Modern British royal family life straddles the 19th century to the present, and working for them gave me a perspective on food and entertaining that fused the historical with the contemporary and got to the very heart of cuisine's place within culture. Dinner parties spanned the gamut, from glittering state affairs in the grand dining halls at Buckingham Palace to shooting parties held in unheated barns with guests passing around their hip flasks to anyone who wanted a nip. It was a royal display of the richness of home life.

In a decidedly more common vein, I grew up with a mother who loved cooking and entertaining, and my parents often hosted dinners. Mum's parties were so good that all her friends teased and asked, "Can we give you money for the food and you host all the parties?" With their cut glass cocktail pitchers, sparkling glasses of Babycham with glace cherries in the bottom, and wreaths of cigarette smoke in the air, my parents seemed awfully glamorous to me. My mother looked beautiful, chatting with friends, drink in hand with its telltale red lipstick stain on the rim. She was known among her set as a very good cook, and my parents' parties were always friendly affairs with simple, delicious food to go along. Mum taught us that you don't need to have a reason for a party, just a sense of fun.

When I got older and rented my first flat, I'd invite friends (mostly other chefs) round for dinners. Sometimes I laid out cheese platters and charcuterie plates with lots of beer. Other times we would emulate the Savoy, preparing dishes off the menu. Those dinners, served with plenty of wine and riotous conversation lasted well into the night. By evening's end the candles would be nearly burnt out, the table was littered with bread crumbs and empty bottles and there was the lingering scent of a well cooked dinner. I'd look at all that and decide that the dirty dishes could wait until tomorrow!

Great evenings are homemade affairs. It's around the dinner table with friends where we laugh, toast, share and connect. We break bread with one another and in doing so cast an invisible thread bringing us closer together. I wrote this book to encourage you to cast that thread more often. Invite friends over. Light the candles, chill down a few bottles, have something wonderful braising in the oven. Set another place at the table (or two or three) and drink, talk, eat and talk some more!

Unlike royal family dinners, entertaining at home doesn't require a larder stocked with foie gras or truffles, restaurant style ovens or hired help. At our house the formal linen and crystal are dispensed with in favor of woven placements and ordinary silverware. When I entertain friends, I want to make people feel welcome. I surely don't want to add stress to anyone's life, mine included.

To help, I've put together a well edited and seasonal selection of menus with foolproof, great tasting dishes. This is, I think, much more helpful than another hefty tome with 1,001 recipes to slog through as you try to look for inspiration. I'm also attracted to the notion that it is far better to cook simple dishes you love and which work well than complicated dishes of dubious origin from glossy magazines. Food shouldn't be a distraction or take over. Its preparation should not be a herculean task which leaves the cook frazzled and spent. Food for family and friends should smell and taste great. That's all. Really, can you imagine a Michelin star chef with his tweezers trying to neatly arrange a crab and shrimp boil that had just been upturned onto a table covered in newspaper?

Now here is where my first maxim comes in: To eat well, you must learn to cook. Sorry, but there is no way around this one. But here is the good news—cooking isn't hard! It's a craft that anyone can learn to do and do well. A freshly made salad with an interesting variety of lettuces, herbs and a simple vinaigrette is always much better than a pre-washed bagged salad with a bottle of commercial dressing. If you have good ingredients on hand, your job is already halfway done. Add easy-to-follow techniques and a reasonable number of ingredients, and you'll find the distance between start and finish pleasurably brief.

During my years of teaching cooking classes, I've noticed a growing lack of confidence among home cooks, especially when it comes to entertaining. My advice is this: Don't forget the great home cooks you've known. They were mothers, fathers, aunts, grandmothers, or even close family friends. They entertained frequently, often with great style and always with food everyone loved. Not a few could even turn the most ordinary ingredients into wonderful tasting fare. I remember my grandfather coming home from the factory, putting on his old clothes and heading out to his allotment. Maybe it was the way he nurtured his rhubarb, carrots, onions, leeks and potatoes, but his yield from that tiny plot was astonishing. The whole family respected the produce he brought to the kitchen. Fresh, local and organic. Not to mention, economical, resourceful and creative too.

That's a good thing to remember. Entertaining doesn't have to be fancy. Stiff, ritualized dinner parties with elaborate cutlery are for the most part long gone, and thank goodness for that. When I first moved to the States, I wanted to impress some new friends and sent out invitations to a dinner party at my house. Everyone accepted and I spent weeks fine tuning the menu, polishing my crystal, silver dipping my flatware, deciding which china would best suit the menu, even making sure I had the right soup bowls for the soup course. After all, one simply can't serve a veloute soup in a consommé cup, I reasoned. My guests loved the food, the evening too, but it wasn't until later I realized how uncomfortable they must have been sitting through six courses, wondering whether this was a fish knife or salad knife course and so on. I resolved never to do that to guests again.

Today we are free to express ourselves, be creative and entertain in a way that builds upon our strengths. I love the way some of my friends entertain. One is a committed gardener, and we start dinner by picking it first (most of it anyway). It's actually a lot of fun. I understand now why Queen Elizabeth and her sister used to spend time bent over the raspberry canes at Balmoral Castle picking berries for dinner. Another friend of mine loves dessert and indulges her love of all things sweet by hosting summer teas. Then there are the wine lovers, and those parties seem to last way into the night...

I hope the menus in this book inspire you to create memorable evenings of your own. The recipes are delicious, relatively simple and include plenty of "work ahead" strategies to calm the fearful chef inside you and allow you to bring impressive meals to the table without wishing you had a professional line cook in the kitchen pinch hitting for the evening. Even the most formal parties at my house seem to always start with guests standing in the kitchen chatting. Also, nothing here is fixed in stone and you should feel free to substitute a dish or ingredient that you prefer.

I've organized the books in a seasonal format. It's meant to be helpful in two ways; the seasonal menus should make shopping a little easier (and cheaper), and it can provide a simple illustration of how I like to put a meal together. Of course, use that as a general guide, not a commandment, and feel free to range as far and wide as your creative juices allow.

From brunch to lunch to tea to dinner and beyond, these menus can provide a solid base from which you can begin exploring and enjoying all of life's momentous, and not so momentous, occasions.

SPRING

There have been poems, songs and sonnets written about the beauty of spring but I've never understood it. In the north of England, spring means less snow, more mud and rain, until seemingly within a week, every tree suddenly blooms. Time lapse photography of spring in Nottinghamshire would come in under fifteen seconds. In Texas where I live, there is such a thing as spring, but we call it winter. By March the temperature is already in the high '70s, low '80s with cloudless skies. Pleasant to be outside for sure, but you can already project in your mind's eye just how hot the next few months will be.

For much of southern England though, spring can be glorious. The tantalizing promise of sunshine comes with budding wild primroses, Canterbury bells and Michaelmas daisies followed by sweet pea blossoms, ranunculas, ever present phlox and masses of forsythia with its sprays of yellow blooms. I remember the bouquets of cut flowers that would be harvested from the gardens at Windsor Castle and arranged into magnificent displays in large ornate urns along the wide hallways and through the royal apartments.

Perhaps it's because I am a chef that I do notice flowers quite a bit, especially the edible ones, like nasturtiums, that automatically brighten up my salad and dessert plates. It's that combination of colors and textures that reminds me when plating a dinner that you do indeed "eat with your eyes first." Food, like flowers, should always look good. Each spring, my catering company in Dallas "Eating Royally, Fine Dining" cooks for numerous charity events and philanthropic fundraisers, so it is important that I make sure everything from tables to flowers to food looks its best.

I've been connected to charity and philanthropic circles nationwide for a long time, sometimes as a chef and caterer, but often as someone donating their services to charitable causes. Participating in philanthropy was something I learned from the world's best teacher, Princess Diana.

It was "the Boss" and her ceaseless support of charities at home and abroad who showed me the importance of good works. As her personal chef at Kensington Palace, I remember being asked along with several of my chef friends to donate our time to help pull off an event for an organization called Children in Need. Working on our day off? For no pay? We all turned up our noses. But watching the Princess' unwavering commitment to needy children, the sick and the elderly inspired me to start doing the same. At that time she was patron to 119 charities... surely I could "do my bit" even for just one! After her death I continued supporting her favorite charity, donating the advance and royalties from my first cookbook *Eating Royally: Recipes and Remembrances from a Palace Kitchen* to the Elizabeth Glaser Pediatric AIDS Foundation. Given that Princess Diana's focus was on children and AIDS, this seemed to bring both together nicely. Currently I support American charities like the American Cancer Society, the American Heart Association, a local Dallas based suicide and crisis center and a number of children's charities. It's all thanks to the Princess: she left an important legacy of giving back and it's one I'm proud to see her sons, William and Harry, continuing in their own lives.

So each spring my personal and business calendar starts filling up with both fundraising parties and "fun"raising parties. On the "fun" side, there is Easter, St. Paddy's Day and

"Carry out a random act of kindness, with no expectation of reward, safe in the knowledge that one day someone might do the same for you."

– Princess Diana –

Mother's Day—all holidays we celebrate in the UK much the same as in the States. One of my favorites though is the Kentucky Derby, held in early May, which reminds me of the Royal Ascot races and Derby Day at Epsom. The Queen, who's passionate about horse racing, always attends both. A much younger me and my mates would prepare the Royal hampers for the Royal Box at each racecourse and then wander around the grounds, placing bets and confirming that yes, horse racing did indeed attract the most beautiful "fillies" per square meter than any other place on earth!

Even though I live in Texas my cooking during the season remains rooted in my remembrances of English spring time. I yearn for the Jersey Royal potatoes back home. They have a unique flavor that comes from a combination of the island of Jersey's rich fertile soil and layers of seaweed used as fertilizer. Rinsed under cold water to wash away any mud and never peeled but boiled with a large spring of mint and seasoned while hot with sea salt and cracked pepper and drizzled with Cornish butter they shout, "spring has arrived!" There are fresh English peas and thin and thick spears of asparagus, both served simply and with a good lashing of sweet butter. I collect lots of early lettuces from the garden that go right into the salad bowl, drizzled with olive oil and a touch of balsamic vinegar. Small, intensely sweet local strawberries, the first of the season, show up in lots of ways, usually paired with freshly whipped Chantilly cream, a favorite of my wife and son. Come Sunday dinner, a joint of roast lamb is very much appreciated in our household served with mint sauce and roasted tiny new potatoes. A slice of lemon tart for dessert, citrusy and tangy, looks like sunshine on a plate.

Spring never seems to last very long and sometimes the busyness of life blinkers us. But subtly at first and then with a shout, nature opens up in full bloom. The beauty and bounty of the farms and gardens around me provide the perfect entry into seasonal entertaining with menus that use local produce and underscore the maxim, "What grows together, goes together."

A CHILDREN'S EASTER EGG ROLL

Chocolate and Easter are a happy pairing; a sweet celebration after forty days of Lent. When I worked in the Royal household, we chefs labored to create all sorts of tempting chocolate treats for the Queen, who had given up her favorite Bendicks Bittermints and Charbonel et Walker chocolates as part of her Lenten observation. We made handcrafted chocolate eggs created from dark chocolate, the darker the chocolate the better for Her Majesty. Of course we used milk chocolate and white chocolate too... but for the royal nursery. Chocolate cakes of all kinds were baked, especially her favorites like chocolate biscuit cake, chocolate perfection pie, Whisky chocolate mousse and a sunken chocolate soufflé called Andrassy pudding. There were also some traditional English cakes, like Simnel cake, a kind of light fruitcake with marzipan that dates back to medieval times. We Brits love our fruit cakes.

My wife and I bring a bit of England to Texas with our annual Easter Egg Roll. The tradition of rolling eggs on grass goes back hundreds of years in England and when I was growing up, it wasn't done with chocolate eggs, but real, hard boiled ones. The eggs were traditionally wrapped in onion skins and boiled to color them a light gold color which made them easier to see in the grass. Armed with long- handled kitchen spoons, we would compete to see who could roll their egg the furthest. It seems that kids in Texas enjoy this game as much as I did. What a reprieve for little ones all dressed in their Sunday best to let loose and race around the grass trying to find out who has won. Of course, a large decorated chocolate egg goes to the victor.

Easter should be a sweet moment for children and adults alike. Cakes, chocolates, jellies and puddings are a perfectly fine lunch once a year.

GANACHE CHOCOLATE EGG CAKES

THIS IS A GREAT RECIPE FOR THE BUDDING PASTRY ENTHUSIAST. The cakes start with a traditional chocolate sponge filled with dark chocolate ganache and rolled up. The roll is then sliced and the individual slices are covered with more ganache and finally decorated. They are a chocolate lover's delight. Be prepared that once you make them, they will be on your "to do" list for every subsequent Easter. You've been warned. MAKES ABOUT 12 CAKES

FOR THE FILLING
2 (4 ounce) bars Ghirardelli dark chocolate

1 cup heavy cream

FOR THE SPONGE
1 tablespoon butter—melted, for greasing

¼ cup flour—for dusting

8 egg yolks

8 egg whites

1 ½ cups granulated sugar

½ cup + 3 tablespoons potato starch (don't use cornstarch)

½ cup Dutch cocoa

¼ cup granulated sugar—for dusting the parchment

FOR THE TOPPING
4 (4 ounce) bars Ghirardelli dark chocolate

2 cups heavy cream

DECORATION
1 large bag Cadbury chocolate mini eggs

1 tablespoon powdered sugar

1 tablespoon cocoa powder

1 Prepare the filling by melting the chocolate. Bring the cream to a boil in a heavy pan and whisk into the melted chocolate until combined. Leave to cool overnight on the counter, unless it's a really hot night then pop it in the fridge. If you do refrigerate it, you will need to let it come back to room temperature the next day to soften up to a spreadable consistency. (Note: refrigerating the ganache makes it more matte in appearance and you will lose that lovely shine).

2 Next, make the sponge. Preheat the oven to 350°F. Line a baking sheet with parchment paper and brush the top with the melted butter, then lightly dust with the flour. In a large bowl, beat the egg yolks with the sugar until pale and fluffy. In a separate bowl beat the egg whites until stiff. In another bowl, sift the potato starch and cocoa together and blend together.

3 Add half of the egg whites to the yolk mix and fold in, then the cocoa mix and the remaining egg white. Pour onto the prepared tray and spread out to the edges. Bake for about 15 minutes or until the sponge springs back when touched.

4 Lay out a large sheet of parchment paper and dust with the ¼ cup sugar. Turn out the sponge onto the parchment, remove the top layer of parchment and allow to cool.

5 Spread the filling over the sponge and roll up. Slice into 1 inch thick pieces and lay on a cooling rack with a sheet of parchment or a cookie tray underneath

6 Prepare the topping the same way as the filling in step 1. Ladle the warm ganache over the tops of each sponge and allow to cool. Make a nest with the remaining topping mix and place three mini chocolate eggs on top of each sponge. Dust with the powdered sugar and cocoa.

» Ganache Chocolate Egg Cakes, page 18

PEANUT BUTTER & JELLY MUFFINS

I CREATED THIS RECIPE WHEN I WORKED AT KENSINGTON PALACE. William and Harry had just come back from visiting Disney World with their mother and had a newfound love for peanut butter and jelly. This recipe makes delicious muffins with a surprise peanut butter and jelly center, great for Easter and any other Sunday morning when you have a few minutes to spare. MAKES 12

2 cups flour

⅔ cup sugar

2 ½ teaspoons baking powder

¼ teaspoon soda

½ teaspoon salt

1 cup milk

½ cup butter—melted and cooled slightly

2 eggs

½ teaspoon vanilla paste or extract

1 cup peanut butter—crunchy

1 cup strawberry jam

1 Preheat the oven to 400°F. Grease a 12 cup muffin tray. Add the flour, sugar, baking powder, salt and soda to a large bowl and mix well

2 In a second bowl mix the milk, butter, egg and vanilla paste. Add the dry ingredients to the milk/butter mixture and stir together. Divide the batter between the muffin tins and add a tablespoon of peanut butter followed by a tablespoon of Jelly to the center each muffin.

3 Bake in the center of the oven until the muffins are golden brown.

SIMNEL CAKE

SIMNEL CAKE IS A VERY LIGHT FRUITCAKE WITH AN ABUNDANCE OF RAISINS, EITHER GOLDEN RAISINS CALLED SULTANAS, REGULAR DARK RAISINS OR SMALL ZANTE CURRANTS, WHICH ARE ALSO RAISINS BUT WHICH COME FROM VERY SMALL GRAPES. This cake, heavy with fruit, almond paste and brandy, keeps very well and actually improves with age. Just wrap it up tightly so it doesn't dry out between nibbles. MAKES ABOUT 12 PORTIONS

3 cups sultanas

2 lemons—zest and juice

2 oranges—zest and juice

3 tablespoons brandy—optional

2 sticks unsalted butter—softened

1 cup + 2 tablespoons granulated sugar

4 eggs

1 ¾ cups self rising flour

1 teaspoon ground cinnamon

1 teaspoon nutmeg

2 (7 ounce) containers almond paste/marzipan

½ cup apricot jelly

1 Preheat the oven to 350°F. Grease an 8 inch by 2 ½ inch round cake ring or pan and line the bottom with parchment paper.

2 In a large bowl add the sultanas, orange and lemon zest and juice and optional brandy. Cover and leave to soak. These can be soaked for up to 24 hours and give a more intense flavor.

3 Cream the butter and sugar until pale and gradually beat in the eggs. Fold in the flour, cinnamon and nutmeg and then add the marinated fruit. Stir and place half of the mix into the cake ring.

4 Roll out one of the tubes of almond paste to about ¼ inch thick and into a circle the size of the cake ring—save the trimmings. Lay it on top of the cake mix in the cake ring and cover with the rest of the cake mix.

5 Bake at 350°F for about 2 hours. If the top starts to darken, cover with aluminum. Remove to a cooling rack and allow to cool. (This stage can be done up to 4 weeks ahead and the cakes can be wrapped tightly and stored in a cool place).

6 Remove the cake from its ring or pan and roll out the remaining tube of almond paste to fit the top of the cake. Save the trimmings. Heat the apricot jelly and brush over the top of the cake and lay the almond paste on top.

7 Form 12 balls with the almond paste trimmings and arrange around the edge of the cake. Place under a high broiler for about three minutes or use a Brulee torch until the almond paste is a golden brown. Finish the cake with a yellow ribbon around the side tied in a bow and serve.

» *Healthy Turkey Meatloaf, page 24,*
and Fat Free Potato Wedges, page 25

SPRING BREAK WITH THE KIDS ALL HOME

My daughter Kelly called the other night to let us know she was heading out to get her laundry done before her flight home for spring break. "Just checking in to see what you are planning on cooking while I'm home," she chirped. "I definitely want Thai food but if not, can we go to that Indian place? I'm open to either. Also for breakfast, your eggs benedict would be fantastic. Are you going to make me a banana cake? Please say yes. Hey let's do Sunday dinner. It's ages since I've had Yorkshire Puddings." By the time I hung up the phone I felt like I'd taken a catering order from one of my clients.

I shouldn't complain, especially since I did the exact same thing to my Mum when I was younger. I was always asking for my favorite dishes like "Liver a la Francaise" a dish she learned in a culinary course. Layers of beef liver in a casserole dish topped with a breadcrumb mix of bacon, onions and herbs and braised in chicken broth... it is so good that I still ask for it today. Another favorite was her beef stew and dumplings; tender chunks of beef and vegetables in gravy with fluffy dumplings floating like clouds on top. Come to think of it, that might have been my Grandmother's recipe because she used to make the same dish, though between Mum and my Nan, it was best to steer clear of who "owned" what recipe. There was also smoked haddock with creamy mashed potatoes and peas, ultimate comfort food that I could never get enough of. I think Mum must have been sick of making those dishes for me, but that lovely woman never complained. She was just happy to have her children back home.

With everyone under the same roof, it is time to cook all their favorites. For us it will be English flapjacks in the morning, and comfort food like meatloaf and potatoes for dinner. Of course there will be caramel banana cake. It is Kelly's favorite... and mine too.

HEALTHY TURKEY MEATLOAF

MADE WITH GROUND TURKEY AND OATS, THIS IS A MOIST, FLAVORFUL MEATLOAF WHICH IS ALSO A LOT HEALTHIER THAN A TRADITIONAL GROUND BEEF OR BEEF/PORK LOAF.
MAKES 6 PORTIONS

FOR THE MEATLOAF
2 pounds ground turkey

1 ½ teaspoon kosher salt

½ teaspoon black pepper

4 cloves garlic, crushed

2 teaspoons dried oregano

1 cup onion, finely chopped

1 cup bell pepper, finely chopped

2 eggs

1 (14 ounce) can diced tomatoes, including the juice

1 cup old fashioned quick cooking oats

FOR THE TOPPING
1 cup tomato ketchup

2 tablespoons yellow mustard

2 tablespoons brown sugar

1 Preheat the oven to 350°F. Place all of the meatloaf ingredients into a large bowl and mix well. Grease a baking sheet and form the mix into one large loaf on the baking sheet.

2 Whisk together the topping ingredients and spoon over the top of the meatloaf. Bake in the center of the oven for about 45 minutes. Cool before slicing.

FAT FREE POTATO WEDGES

IF YOUR FAMILY IS LIKE OURS, MEATLOAF AND POTATO WEDGES ARE ALWAYS BIG FAVORITES. These potatoes, coated in egg white instead of oil deliver plenty of flavor yet keep the calories under control. MAKES 4 PORTIONS

6 medium Yukon Gold potatoes, about 2 pounds

2 teaspoons smoked paprika

1 teaspoon fresh minced garlic

1 teaspoon sea salt

½ teaspoon ground black pepper

1 egg white

1 Preheat the oven to 400°F. Cut the potatoes into wedges by cutting each potato in half lengthways and then each half into four and place in a large bowl.

2 Add the paprika, garlic, salt and pepper to the potatoes. Beat the egg white in a small bowl and add to the potatoes and toss to coat.

3 Spread the potatoes on a baking sheet and bake in the center of the oven, turning halfway through cooking for about 30 minutes or golden brown and soft in the center.

ENGLISH FLAPJACKS

THESE COOKIES NEED TO BE CUT RIGHT AFTER YOU TAKE THEM OUT OF THE OVEN. That's important. The golden syrup makes them quite firm as they cool so don't wait. One last piece of advice: don't overcook them. MAKES 12 FLAPJACKS

3 sticks unsalted butter

3 tablespoons golden syrup

1 ½ cups granulated sugar

1 cup + 1 tablespoon self rising flour

2 cups old fashioned rolled oats

3 cups cornflakes

½ teaspoon salt

1 Preheat the oven to 350°F. Lightly grease a 12x9x1 baking tray.

2 Melt the butter and golden syrup over a low heat but do not boil. Add the sugar and combine. Stir in the self rising flour, oats, salt and cornflakes and stir until the cornflakes are all covered with the butter syrup mix.

3 Spoon onto the prepared baking tray and flatten. Bake in the center of the oven for about 20 minutes or until the flapjacks are a golden brown. Remove from the oven and cool slightly. Cut into fingers while still warm and allow to cool completely before serving.

CARAMEL BANANA CAKE

BANANA AND CARAMEL GO GREAT TOGETHER AND THIS CAKE NEVER SEEMS TO LAST LONGER THAN A DAY IN MY HOUSE. It's perfect with a strong cup of tea. MAKES 24 BARS

FOR THE CAKE

½ cup + 2 teaspoons butter, for greasing the pan

¾ cups light brown sugar

2 eggs

1 cups mashed bananas (about 3 small)

1 ½ cups self rising flour

1 teaspoon baking soda

¾ cup sour cream

1 tablespoon milk

1 teaspoon vanilla paste or extract

FOR THE FROSTING

¾ cup unsalted butter

1 cup light brown sugar

¼ cup sour cream

3 cups powdered sugar

1 teaspoon vanilla paste or extract

1 Preheat the oven to 350°F. Grease a sheet pan tray (9 ½ x 13).

2 Prepare the cake by creaming the butter and sugar using an electric mixer until light and fluffy. Add the eggs and banana and beat together. Stir in the flour, soda, sour cream, milk and vanilla paste until there are no lumps and the batter is smooth.

3 Pour into the prepared tray and bake in the center of the oven for about 40 minutes or until the cake springs back when touched and is a golden brown.

4 Allow the cake to cool completely before frosting.

5 Prepare the frosting by melting the butter and sugar in a pan. Stir without boiling for about 2 minutes. Add the sour cream, bring to a boil. Remove from the heat and stir in the powdered sugar and vanilla paste. Leave the frosting to cool slightly and thicken before carefully frosting the cake. Cut into fingers and serve.

» Black Bean & Shucked Corn Salad, page 30;
Chili Con Carnitas, page 31;
Garlic Chicken Drumsticks with a Honey, Lemon Glaze, page 32;
and Mini Beef Sliders with a Bacon & Beet Aioli, page 33

MARCH MADNESS

The NCAA tournaments are an American tradition that sends millions of fans into a synchronized frenzy each year. It's this chaos that gives the tournament its March Madness nickname. An original 68 teams are winnowed down to an elite foursome called "the Final Four" leading to the final competition that will crown an NCAA champion. Now that I've impressed you with my paltry grasp of March Madness fundamentals, let me tell you what it really is to me—the basketball equivalent of the Superbowl, which I love!

Since the final NCAA game is often held on a Monday, heavy drinking is usually down to a minimum. Beer suffices. I also like keeping food easy to manage and finger friendly. After all, most eyes are on the TV screen, not on managing to keep a plate from wobbling off your knee while you try to cut a piece of chicken. One handed bites like chicken drumsticks and mini burgers are always a good choice and, here in Texas, there is usually something spicy on the menu like mini tacos. I love Mexican flavors with plenty of punch that wake up your taste buds and go great with beer. Given how fast my guests eat my chili, I suppose I'm not the only one. For game viewing, I like to serve food on large trays and people can just help themselves. No worrying if the food isn't piping hot; it's just as good warm or at room temperature. Load up your coffee table with platters, napkins and beer, find a spot on the couch and game on!

BLACK BEAN & SHUCKED CORN SALAD

I CALL THIS A SALAD BECAUSE OFTEN I SERVE IT ON A BED OF CHOPPED ROMAINE WITH CHICKEN OR PORK. But when I have friends over this dish becomes a grown up salsa instead. Serve in a large bowl with plenty of tortilla chips for scooping. MAKES 4 PORTIONS

4 corn on the cob, shucked and brushed with oil

1 (15 ounce) can black beans, drained

½ cup finely diced red onion

½ cup chopped fresh cilantro

1 jalapeño pepper, seeded and finely diced

2 ripe avocados, diced into bite size pieces

1 orange bell pepper, seeded and diced

2 cups San Marzano cherry tomatoes (you can use regular cherry tomatoes) halved

¼ cup extra virgin olive oil

½ teaspoon ground cumin

1 clove garlic, minced

2 tablespoons freshly squeezed lime juice

1 tablespoon agave syrup (or honey)

Salt and pepper to taste

1 Grill the corn until golden or place over a naked flame on the stove turning until it has a nice golden color. Cool the corn and then carefully remove from the husk.

2 Place the corn along with the black beans, red onion, cilantro, jalapeño, avocado, bell pepper and tomatoes into a large bowl and mix.

3 In a small bowl whisk the olive oil, cumin, garlic, lime juice and agave syrup until combined and smooth and pour over the salad. Mix until coated and season with salt and pepper.

4 Serve in a large bowl over chopped romaine or in a serving dish with some crostini or tortilla chips for scooping.

CHILI CON CARNITAS

THIS IS A GREAT RECIPE FOR PARTIES. BY COMBINING TWO RECIPES, CHILI AND CARNITAS, THE PORK STAYS MOIST LONGER AND IS SO GOOD SPOONED INTO SOFT FLOUR OR CORN TORTILLAS. Serve alongside a bowl of lime wedges, some salsa, sour cream and lots of fresh roughly chopped cilantro. Your guests will definitely be coming back for seconds.

Traditionally carnitas are cooked slowly in a skillet on the stove. But when I am making this dish, out comes my electric pressure cooker. Forty five minutes on high and you have the most tender carnitas and delicious sauce ever. MAKES 4 PORTIONS (WITH SOME FOR SECONDS)

3 pounds boneless pork shoulder, cut into large cubes

½ cup chili powder (or to taste)

1 tablespoon ground cumin

1 orange, zest and juice

2 bay leaves

1 teaspoon dried oregano

1 (12 ounce) bottle Mexican beer

1 onion, chopped

1 jalapeño, seeded and chopped

4 cloves of garlic, crushed

1 dried chipotle chili (optional)

2 (15 ounce) cans diced tomatoes

2 chicken bouillon cubes

Salt and pepper to taste

1 At least 4 hours before (I like to do this 24 hours before to intensify the flavor) put the pork, chili powder, cumin, orange zest and juice, bay leaf, oregano, beer, onion, jalapeño, garlic and chipotle chili into a ziplock bag. Seal the bag and massage the meat with the other ingredients.

2 Add the meat and marinade to the skillet or pressure cooker along with the diced tomatoes and bouillon cubes and bring to a boil. Place the lid on the pressure cooker, seal and set the pressure on high for 45 minutes until the meat is fork tender and just falling apart a bit. If you choose to cook on the stove you will need to let the meat simmer in the skillet, covered for at least two hours.

3 Once cooked, remove the chipotle chili and discard. Season with salt and pepper before serving.

GARLIC CHICKEN DRUMSTICKS WITH A HONEY, LEMON GLAZE

SERVES 4

8 chicken drumsticks

FOR THE RUB
3 teaspoons garlic powder
¼ teaspoon ground black pepper
2 teaspoons kosher salt
3 tablespoons olive oil

FOR THE GLAZE
¼ cup honey
1 tablespoon sesame oil
Juice of 1 lemon
1 clove crushed garlic
Pinch salt
2 splashes Louisiana hot sauce

½ cup chopped cilantro

1 Preheat the oven to 400°F. Score the chicken drumsticks by cutting into the flesh ½ inch deep several times. Place the garlic powder, black pepper, salt and olive oil in a large bowl and add the chicken drumsticks. Mix until well coated. Place the chicken onto a large baking sheet and bake for 30-40 minutes. Do not turn the chicken. Remove from the oven when cooked and allow to cool slightly.

2 Prepare the glaze by bringing the honey, sesame oil, lemon juice and garlic to a boil in a heavy based pan. Whisk until combined and boil for about three minutes until the consistency of maple syrup. Remove from the heat and add the salt and hot sauce.

3 Turn the chicken upside down and glaze using a pastry brush. Garnish with the chopped cilantro. Serve crispy side up with the additional glaze served alongside. I only glaze one side for a punch of flavor while keeping the chicken leg crispy.

MINI BEEF SLIDERS WITH BACON & BEET AIOLI

BEEF SLIDERS ARE THE ULTIMATE COCKTAIL PARTY FOOD. This recipe takes them to the next level. Princess Diana would often request a bacon and sliced beet sandwich, an unusual but surprisingly good combination. For this dish I use both red beets and golden beets just to add texture and color. This is my go to party recipe when I am entertaining at home and it always has me reaching for my sous-vide machine. I sous vide cook the beets at 185°F for an hour, usually the day before, and then before guests arrive season and sear the beef and sous vide it at 139°F for an hour. All you have to do is just slice and put it on the rolls and serve... delicious! MAKES 8 SLIDERS

1 large golden beet

1 large red beet

½ cup mayonnaise

1 clove garlic, minced

1 teaspoon Sriracha sauce (or to taste)

1 pound beef tenderloin, center cut, seasoned with salt and pepper

8 slices smoked bacon, cooked crisp

½ teaspoon caraway seeds, toasted

2 cups baby arugula

8 slider rolls

2 tablespoons rapeseed oil

1 Place the beets in separate pans of cold water covering them well with the water and boil until fork tender, about 45 minutes. Once cooked run the beets under cold water to cool. Peel the beets using a paper towel if you would like to avoid stained hands!

2 Slice the golden beet into eight thin slices and set aside. Chop the red beet into a food processor and puree until no lumps. In a large bowl add the mayonnaise, garlic and sriracha and gradually add the pureed beet until you have a thick spreadable sauce. Refrigerate until needed.

3 Roast or sous vide your beef tenderloin to desired doneness. If roasting, I like to cook the beef medium rare. Season the beef with salt and pepper and sear in a heavy based skillet once the oil is smoking hot. Place the beef in a 400°F oven for about 20 minutes and rest on a serving plate for at least 10 minutes before slicing.

4 Split the sliders and spread about a tablespoon of the beet aioli onto the bottom bread. Top with a slice of beef, bacon arugula and caraway seeds. Place the slider lid on top and serve.

MOTHER'S DAY BRUNCH

I am going to make a plea to everyone frantically trying to get a restaurant reservation on Mother's Day: just stop the madness. It's crazy that we all feel obliged to take our mothers and wives out for a crowded and loud late breakfast where the waiters are trying to get you in and out in record time so they and the restaurant owners can make as much money as possible. The result? Sadly, too often the food and service are mediocre.

Here's a better suggestion: buy a beautiful bouquet of flowers and put them on your table, get the kids to make a lovely homemade card, grab your and the kid's cell phones and hide them away in a tall cabinet, open a bottle (or two) of prosecco and set out some nice fluted glasses, put on your mother's (or wife's) favorite music—anything from ABBA to The New Seekers to Phil Collins to The Black Eyed Peas, and cook something that she and the whole family loves to eat. It doesn't have to be complicated, fancy or overwrought. Just delicious. Most importantly though, don't forget to raise those glasses of prosecco and tell all the Mum's around your table how much you appreciate all they have done and that you love them. Full stop. Oh, and don't forget the hugs.

ASPARAGUS & GRUYERE FRITTATA

IF YOU HAVE NEVER HAD A FRITTATA BEFORE, THINK OF IT AS BASICALLY A CRUSTLESS QUICHE. If you have, then you will know what all the fuss is about. Vegetables and bits of meat suspended in a fluffy light, egg mixture with a little melted cheese. Not too filling, but substantial enough that you won't need any potatoes or pasta to round out the meal. The secret to a good frittata is to cook all of your vegetables before putting them into your egg mixture. This recipe is vegetarian but feel free to add some cubed chicken, crumbled sausage or bacon for a heartier version. MAKES 4 (GENEROUS) PORTIONS

1 (2 quart) casserole dish

12 eggs
½ cup milk
¼ cup heavy cream

1 teaspoon salt
¼ teaspoon ground black pepper

1 small red onion, sliced and sautéed until soft

1 bunch asparagus, cut into 1-inch pieces, steamed or sautéed alongside the onion
1 cup cherry tomatoes, halved
2 tablespoons fresh chopped dill
1 cup grated Gruyere cheese

1 Preheat the oven to 350°F.

2 In a large bowl beat the eggs, but don't over beat or the frittata will puff like a soufflé and then collapse. Whisk in the milk, cream, salt and pepper.

3 Stir in the cooked asparagus, red onion, tomatoes and dill and pour into the casserole dish. Bake in the center of the oven for about 30 minutes or until a knife inserted into the frittata comes out clean.

4 Remove from the oven and sprinkle the Gruyere cheese over the top of the frittata. Leave in a warm place to set up and for the cheese to melt for about 10 minutes before serving.

» Asparagus & Gruyere Frittata, page 36

PROSCIUTTO WRAPPED HALIBUT WITH CHIPOTLE HOLLANDAISE

WRAPPING DELICATE FISH IN PROSCIUTTO NOT ONLY ADDS A DELICIOUS SWEET AND SALTY FLAVOR, IT ALSO SEALS IN THE MOISTURE. This allows the cooked fish to sit a little longer without drying out. The chipotle hollandaise can be made while the fish is in the oven and is best served in a sauce boat on the side allowing Mom to take as little or as much as she wants.

Hollandaise can be a little finicky to make. For practiced hands it is a quick sauce to whip up at the last minute, sort of like making a warm mayonnaise. But like a mayonnaise, the possibility of the sauce breaking is very real. So, what to do? Keep the ingredients at the same temperature, just warm, but never so hot that your eggs start to curdle. Keep a small piece of ice cube at the ready to whisk into the sauce should it start to look grainy. If the sauce is looking too thick (like a firm mayonnaise consistency), add a splash of hot water to thin. Drip the butter, slowly at first, into the eggs, whisking all the while to create a soft emulsion with good volume. Taste as you go.

MAKES 4 PORTIONS

4 (8 ounce) halibut fillets (about 1-inch thick)	5 egg yolks	1 small chipotle (from a can of chipotles in adobo sauce) minced
8 slices Prosciutto	1 teaspoon water	2 tablespoons chopped fresh cilantro
	3 sticks unsalted butter (melted and skimmed of any whey floating on top)	Salt and pepper to taste
1 large bunch asparagus		1 lime, cut into wedges

1 Preheat the oven to 400°F. Season the halibut with salt and pepper. Wrap two slices of Prosciutto around each piece of halibut. Place on a baking sheet and roast for about 10 minutes until the Prosciutto is crispy and the halibut cooked.

2 Trim the ends off the asparagus and plunge into a pan of boiling salted water. Bring the water back to the boil and remove the asparagus. Keep warm.

3 In a large bowl, whisk the egg yolks and water together over a pan of boiling water for about 2 minutes. Remove the bowl and slowly whisk in the melted butter and chipotle. Season with salt and pepper and stir in the chopped cilantro before serving.

4 Place the warm asparagus neatly onto four serving plates and place a piece of halibut on top. Drizzle a little of the sauce over the top (or serve separately in a sauce boat). Garnish with the lime wedges.

CHILLED LEMON TART

MAKES ABOUT 6-8 PORTIONS

FOR THE PASTRY BASE

½ cup sugar

½ cup + 6 tablespoons butter

½ beaten egg

½ teaspoon vanilla paste or extract

1 teaspoon fresh chopped rosemary

1 ¾ cups all purpose flour

Combine all of the ingredients in a food processor and then wrap in parchment and chill for at least 30 minutes.

FOR THE LEMON FILLING

6 eggs

1 ½ cups granulated sugar

1 cup heavy cream

3 lemons (zest and juice)

1 (6 ounce) container fresh raspberries

1 tablespoon powdered sugar

1 cup heavy cream, whipped stiff

1 Preheat the oven to 350°F.

2 A half an hour before baking, remove your pastry dough from the refrigerator and let it soften slightly at room temperature so it is easier to roll out. Line a 9 inch tart pan with the pastry. Place foil the top of the pastry and weigh it down with dried beans. Par bake the dough for about 10 minutes.

3 While the tart is par baking, prepare the filling; In a large bowl add the eggs and sugar and beat together until well blended. Add the cream and whisk into the egg mix. Then add the lemon juice and zest.

4 Carefully remove the foil holding the dried beans from the pastry. Pour the lemon filling into the tart shell. Carefully return the tart to the oven and bake for a further 30-40 minutes until the filling is just set. Remove tart from the oven and allow it to cool on a rack, then chill in the refrigerator. The filling will firm up as it cools. In a food processor, blend the raspberries with the sugar. Fold the raspberry mixture into freshly whipped creamed and serve the tart topped with the cream.

SPOTLIGHT

Superfoods & Healthy Cooking

Every year it seems there is a new ingredient to try or an old one reinterpreted in a new way. That makes my work interesting though I tend to both embrace and be occasionally skeptical of hot new food "trends." My training taught me to believe that good food is good food always, no matter the era. I do remain strongly in favor of sane eating—bacon just doesn't belong in everything. I was at the store just yesterday and they were sampling ice cream with bacon bits. Yikes!

When people find out that I worked in the Royal kitchens for Queen Elizabeth and then for Princess Diana they think I cooked rich, indulgent food all the time. Quite the opposite. The royal family's good health comes from meals that are largely organic, amazingly local and prepared very simply. Of course, the Royal family still occasionally dined on traditional French recipes, many laden with heavy cream and lots of butter. But they were disciplined and only ate small portions. When I started cooking for Princess Diana I almost had to throw my recipe book out of the palace gates. She had confronted and conquered bulimia (which she had long struggled with) and had her life back on track. She said, "Darren, I want you to take care of the fats and I will burn off the carbs at the gym." I started looking at replacements for cream and butter and with her interest in healthy eating, I was always on the look out for healthy ingredients.

While I am not a slave to nutritional advice, I am interested in food that is both good and good for you. There has been a lot of focus of late on so-called "superfoods" i.e. foods that are nutritionally dense, delivering lots of vitamins and minerals. The Princess would have loved them. Looking through the list each year I'm reminded that we usually already know what good food is. Color is a clue—deep reds in wild salmon and apples, pomegranate seeds and chiles, greens in all leafy vegetables like collard, kale and spinach, and blues in blackberries and blueberries. Even orange and yellow including all kids of citrus and rhizomes like turmeric and ginger are wonderful for a healthy diet.

Grains and pulses are also abundant, varied and interesting. One superfood is quinoa, a south american grain with such a high protein content that it is a feasible protein substitute. Another is lentils, which provide protein and complex carbohydrates—a two for one combo that is both easy and flexible. It's great hot in soups and cold in all sorts of salads. Among seeds, I am really impressed with flax, an ancient seed with documented use as far back as ancient Babylonia. Flax has high levels of Omega 3 fatty acids, plant estrogens and antioxidants. Best of all most grains, seeds and pulses are high in fiber, a plus for good digestion.

There are some new ingredients which help me in the kitchen. Xanthan gum is one of them; a thickening agent which works better than either flour or cornstarch, is gluten free and can be used to set both cold and hot sauces. The gum will yield a shiny, perfectly thickened sauce without requiring additional heating.

When my clients tell me they want to start eating healthy I challenge myself to create new recipes with as many Superfoods in them as possible. Salads are a great place to start. Vary your salads each day and throw away all of the bottles of salad dressing in the fridge. Rapeseed oil (cold pressed – it has half the saturated fat of olive oil, rich in vitamin E and Omega-3) with a little apple cider vinegar and honey make the most delicious healthy dressing. Drizzled over freshly shredded kale, chard or beet leaves and topped with papaya and blueberries with a few walnuts yields a fabulous, healthy appetizer.

Challenge yourself—see how many Superfoods you can eat each day.

A SPRING SHOWER

Births, weddings and funerals. The three events in a person's life where cultural traditions speak loudest. I've seen Hindu weddings where the groom came in on an elephant, Polish weddings where at the last moment, the bride's veil was replaced with a babushka and everyone cried, Greek weddings where 150 guests means it is an intimate affair, Arab weddings where the cake is cut with a fancy sword, and nonconformist hipster weddings where everyone wears their favorite color of Converse! Our wedding traditions are as varied as we are.

That variety also holds true for bridal showers. Generally, a bridal shower is for family and friends to celebrate the upcoming nuptials and get the bride-to-be kitted out for her future home. And home is really at the heart of things. Though some are held in restaurants or social venues, the vast majority of bridal showers are homemade affairs and because you are celebrating a young couple's new marriage, everything is meant to be as pretty as possible, the food included. But there are no hard rules. Bridal showers can be full sit down meals, sociable teas, cocktails and nibbles or a late morning brunch. They are flexible.

The menu I've crafted here keeps the food light and especially healthy. There is a blueberry, kale and quinoa salad hearty enough for vegetarians and colorful enough to look gorgeous on a large platter. The grilled chicken is high in protein and more importantly, low in calories. The veloute packs two nutritional powerhouses together, cauliflower and turmeric, to deliver a colorful dose of health benefits to overscheduled brides. And just to make everyone leave with a little special something, I've included directions to make edible chocolate photo picture frames. Unique and fun, they are a wonderful way for the host to make the bride-to-be feel extra special.

BLUEBERRY, FETA & KALE SALAD

THIS KALE SALAD IS GENTLY SWEET WITH FRESH BLUEBERRIES, CRUNCHY WITH SLICED ALMONDS, SALTY WITH FRESH FETA, AND NUTRITIOUS WITH THE ADDITION OF QUINOA. Shred the kale with a sharp knife or a Cuisinart shredding attachment. SERVES 4

1 cup quinoa

2 cups water

1 large head of kale (about 10-12 ounces) washed

¼ cup olive oil

2 tablespoons lemon juice

1 tablespoon Dijon mustard

1 tablespoon agave syrup

6 ounces fresh blueberries

6 ounces feta cheese

2 tablespoons sliced almonds

Salt and pepper

1 Place the quinoa in a pan with the water and bring to a boil. Stir, reduce the heat to low and place a lid on the pan. Simmer for 10 minutes until the water has been absorbed and the quinoa is cooked. Remove the quinoa and place in a bowl to cool.

2 Finely shred the kale about three fourths of the way down the rib and add to a large bowl. Whisk together the olive oil, lemon juice, agave syrup and Dijon mustard. Add salt and pepper to taste. Pour half on to the salad and massage into the kale until it begins to soften and collapse.

3 Add the blueberries, feta cheese, almonds and sprinkle in the quinoa. Mix gently, adding a touch more dressing, if needed.

4 Spoon the salad onto serving plates and serve with any remaining dressing on the side.

GRILLED CHICKEN WITH SALBITXADA SAUCE

THIS RECIPE, WHICH SCALES UP EASILY TO FEED A CROWD, IS AN EASY-TO-ASSEMBLE DISH WITH A BRIGHT AND HEALTHY SAUCE TO GO ALONG. The chicken can be marinated in advance, seared on top of the stove in a sauté pan and then placed on a large baking sheet and roasted until just cooked through. The marinade calls for a chili and garlic paste (both Huy Fong and Dynasty are two good brands) and coriander seeds which I like to buy at a nearby Indian grocery store where the spices are restocked frequently.

Salbitxada is a chunky, piquant sauce originally from the Catalan region that is related to another Spanish sauce, Romesco. Like Romesco, it goes great with chicken, fish, roasted vegetables and even a nice fresh ball of mozzarella.

NOTE: This recipe calls for skin on chicken breasts. The breast has a layer of fat which, along with the marinade, results in juicy piece of chicken. Speak with your local butcher and have some skin-on chicken breasts set aside for you.

FOR THE CHICKEN AND MARINADE

4 chicken breasts (boneless, but skin on)

4 cloves garlic, peeled

1 teaspoon chili and garlic paste

1 teaspoon coriander seeds

1 teaspoon sea salt

½ cup extra virgin olive oil

1 tablespoon sherry vinegar

2 tablespoons lime juice

2 tablespoons orange juice

FOR THE SALBITXADA SAUCE

3 vine ripe tomatoes, quartered

1 roasted red pepper, seeds and stalk removed

½ cup blanched almonds toasted, roughly chopped

½ teaspoon dried red chili flakes

½ teaspoon paprika

3 cloves garlic peeled, crushed

1 teaspoon finely grated lemon zest

2 tablespoons chopped fresh parsley

1 tablespoon sherry vinegar

125ml extra virgin olive oil

Continued on next page...

1 **FOR THE CHICKEN** Flatten out with the palm of your hand, then slash the chicken breast in a few places (skin side) with a sharp knife. Place the chicken into a dish, cover and set aside in the fridge.

2 In a food processor blend the garlic, chilli, coriander seeds, olive oil, sherry vinegar, lime juice and orange juice. Season with salt and black pepper, then pour the mixture over the chicken and leave to marinate in the fridge for at least one hour.

3 **FOR THE SALBITXADA SAUCE** Pulse all of the ingredients to a chunky puree in a food processor and set aside.

4 Pat dry the chicken breasts with paper towel and either grill or pan fry until cooked (about 10 minutes depending on size). Place onto a serving dish and drizzle the Salbitxada sauce over the top just before serving.

TURMERIC CAULIFLOWER VELOUTE

THIS VELOUTE IS A LUXURIOUS MASH OF CAULIFLOWER, ENRICHED WITH CHEESE, BACON AND A TOUCH OF TRUFFLE OIL AND BRIGHTENED WITH TURMERIC TO A GORGEOUS SHADE A YELLOW. SERVES 4 PORTIONS

1 large cauliflower, green stalks removed

1 (8 ounce) pack cream cheese, at room temperature

A pinch of xanthan gum (see note below)

1 teaspoon ground turmeric

¼ cup cooked, crumbled bacon

¼ cup pecorino cheese, freshly grated

1 teaspoon white truffle oil

1 Cut the cauliflower into florets and chop the stalk into small pieces. Boil a large pan of salted water, add the cauliflower and cook until tender. Drain into a colander and pat dry with paper towels. Blend in a food processer until smooth. Add the cream cheese and the pinch of xanthan gum and blend until combined. Season with salt and pepper and turmeric and spoon into a serving dish. Garnish with the crumbled bacon, pecorino and truffle oil before serving.

Note: Xanthan Gum is a common thickening agent which has the added benefit of making sauces shine beautifully. It is a derived from sugar, is gluten free, and gives this cauliflower veloute a lovely consistency. You can find it in most supermarkets, Walmart and online.

CHOCOLATE PICTURE FRAMES

CHOCOLATE PICTURE FRAMES ARE COMPLETELY EDIBLE AND A UNIQUE GIFT TO HAND OUT AT A BRIDAL OR BABY SHOWER. True, they are a little more advanced than most of the recipes in this book but are a great DIY project for someone who loves crafts and chocolate! You will need to source plastic mold frames either online or at a local cake decorating shop, along with edible silver or gold powder. The edible photo can be sourced at Walmart or your local large supermarket in the bakery department. I've included some step by step photos to guide you along.

MAKES 4 PICTURE FRAMES

CHOCOLATE PICTURE FRAME
8 ounces semi sweet chocolate chips

4 plastic chocolate picture frame molds

¼ cup store bought Royal icing

½ ounce container silver or gold sparkle powder

1 teaspoon vodka

ROLLED SUGAR COOKIES
3 tablespoons unsalted butter, softened

¼ cup granulated sugar

1 egg

¼ teaspoon vanilla extract

1 ¼ cups all-purpose flour

½ teaspoon baking powder

¼ teaspoon salt

4 edible cookie sheet photos to fit plastic frame mold

THE DAY AHEAD OF ASSEMBLING THE FRAMES

1 **Make your Chocolate Frame**

Melt the chocolate over a double boiler and carefully pour into the molds all the way to the top. Refrigerate over night or for about 2 hours or until set.

2 **Reprint your photo**

Once you have determined what photo you want to put into your edible frame you need to upload it to a computer and then reduce the size of the photo so that it fits perfectly into the chocolate picture frame. Take it to the local grocery store bakery or cake decorating supply store and ask them to print four photos. Carefully trim the edible photos so they fit into the frames. Set them aside.

1 Color the Frames

Carefully tease the chocolate out of the molds. Mix together the vodka and silver/gold dust and using a small paintbrush paint the frames so no chocolate is visible. The use of vodka here transforms the powder into paint. After the mold is painted, the alcohol in the vodka dries and dissipates.

Set the painted frames aside and allow to dry fully in a cool place.

2 Make your sugar cookie base

Preheat the oven to 350°F.

In a mixing bowl, cream together the butter and sugar until smooth. Beat in the eggs and vanilla. Stir in the flour, baking powder and salt. Chill the dough for at least one hour to set up hard enough to roll.

Roll out the dough on floured surface to about ½ inch thick. Cut into rectangles the size of each picture frame. Bake 6 to 8 minutes in preheated oven until they start to go golden. Remove from the oven and allow to cool and crisp up. Set aside.

3 Assemble the Picture Frames

Lay the four cookies onto a baking sheet and lightly cover the tops with a thin layer of royal icing. Remove the backing of the photos and carefully place the photo on top of the frosting leaving a little frosting hanging out at the edges. Place the chocolate frame on top and lightly press down. Refrigerate the cookies until the frosting has set.

» *Chili Relleno Con Pollo, page 52,*
and Pomegranate Margarita Granita/Sorbet, page 55

CINCO DE MAYO

Italian cuisine is soulful, taking simple ingredients and just letting them shine; a philosophy that says "I see what you are." French and Chinese cuisines are creative, taking ingredients and transforming them into something knew; an approach more "I wonder what you can become?" But Mexican cuisine, one of the world's greats in my opinion, is ultimately both: extremely soulful and intensely, amazingly creative. Imagine combining ingredients from all over the world like sesame, chiles, chocolate, star anise, black peppercorns, cinnamon, bay leaves, bread, ground corn, clove, and almonds and from this chaos you create mole—a breathtaking achievement. If it was up to me I would designate all Mexican moles as Unesco world heritage treasures!

While I didn't grow up with Mexican food, living in Texas these past twenty years has schooled me, at least a little bit, in Mexican food fundamentals. I won't own up to a greater degree of proficiency than that, in part because Mexican cuisine is so varied and complex. Still most of us can easily handle the delicious basics. I remember a vacation to the coastal city of Ensenada eating fish tacos made by a fisherman with the days catch, full of avocado, salsa, shredded lettuce, onion and cilantro... I was in heaven!

Cinco de Mayo takes place every May 5th and that means big celebrations in Texas where 25% of all Mexican Americans live. Locally there are cultural dance and music events, especially mariachi music festivals, and plenty of eating, drinking and dancing through the night. I approve. Tequila, and its magical cousin Mezcal, aren't limited to drinks alone, but find a way into many of my dishes, including a pomegranate margarita granita that tops off the evening. That keeps everyone cool and mellow and outside on a warm May evening, the music playing and the stars twinkling in the night skies.

CHILI RELLENO CON POLLO

MAKES 4 PORTIONS

4 poblano chiles

1 cup Monterey jack cheese, about 4-6 ounces

2 cups chicken breast, cooked and diced

½ small white onion, chopped

2 cloves garlic

2 tablespoons olive oil

5 Roma tomatoes

1 teaspoon chipotle chili powder

1 tablespoon all-purpose flour

1 teaspoon oregano

½ cup heavy cream

Salt and pepper for seasoning

4 eggs, separated

1 teaspoon cumin seeds

½ teaspoon all-purpose flour

¼ cup all-purpose flour for dusting

2 cups vegetable oil

chopped cilantro, to garnish

1 First, char the chilies to remove the skin. Turn a gas burner on high and using tongues rotate the chilies until they are blackened. Place them in a ziplock bag and seal. The steam will help the skins come off easier.

2 Once cold, remove the chilies and take off the skins. Make a slit in the chilies and remove the seeds. Mix together the cheese and chicken and fill the centers of the chilies. Thread a wooden toothpick into each chili to prevent the filling leaking out. Refrigerate the stuffed chilies until needed.

3 Prepare the sauce. Sauté the onions and garlic in the oil until softened. Put the tomatoes, sautéed onions and garlic, chili powder, flour, oregano, cream and salt and pepper in the blender and blend until smooth. Strain into a small pan and reduce on the stove to desired sauce consistency. Season with salt and pepper and keep warm.

4 Heat the vegetable oil in a large skillet until hot (350°F). While it is heating, whip the egg whites using an electric mixer until stiff. In a separate bowl, beat the egg yolks with the cumin seeds and flour. Fold the egg whites into the yolk mixture.

5 Roll the stuffed chilies in the flour and dip in the egg white mix. Carefully place into the oil and cook until golden brown. Turn the chilies over to cook on all sides (about 6 minutes) Remove to a serving platter and garnish with chopped cilantro.

GREEN CHILI CHICKEN & BLACK BEAN ENCHILADAS

THIS IS PROBABLY ONE OF THE MOST POPULAR DISHES ON MY EATING ROYALLY CATERING MENU HERE IN DALLAS AND WHILE THE RECIPE BELOW IS FOR FOUR SERVINGS, THIS SCALES UP EASILY TO SERVE A CROWD. Beautiful corn tortillas stuffed to the brim with chicken, cheese and black beans and smothered in a yummy green chili sauce topped with more cheese and sour cream. What says Cinco de Mayo more than that! MAKES 4 PORTIONS

1 (15 ounce) can black beans, drained

2 tablespoons fresh chopped cilantro

1 tablespoon sriracha chili sauce

2 teaspoons fresh lime juice

2 teaspoons fresh garlic, minced

1 large yellow onion, diced

4 cloves garlic, minced

2 jalapeño peppers, seeded and chopped

8 poblano peppers, seeded and chopped

2 green bell peppers, seeded and chopped

1 pound fresh tomatillos, husks removed

1 bunch cilantro, rough chopped

1 cup chicken broth

8 corn tortillas

1 cup vegetable oil

2 cups Mozzarella cheese

2 cups chicken breast, cooked and shredded

½ cup sour cream

½ cup Monterey jack cheese

½ cup chopped fresh cilantro

1 Add the black beans, cilantro, sriracha, lime juice and garlic to a food processor and pulse until blended. Season with salt and pepper. Set aside.

2 Sauté the yellow onion and garlic in a heavy pan until soft and translucent. Add the onions and garlic to a blender with the jalapeño, poblano and bell peppers, tomatillos, cilantro and chicken broth and blend until smooth. Set aside.

3 Heat the vegetable oil in a large skillet and cook the tortillas until soft and pliable. Dry with paper towel and stuff with the chicken, black beans and cheese and roll. Place in a casserole dish, seam side down, and cover with the green tomatillo sauce. Top with the sour cream and cheese and bake at 350°F for about 15-20 minutes until the cheese has melted and the chicken is hot. Garnish with the chopped cilantro before serving.

CHARRO BEANS

IF YOU DON'T OWN AN ELECTRIC PRESSURE COOKER THEN THIS IS THE RECIPE THAT WILL MAKE YOU RUSH OUT AND BUY ONE. And you will be glad you did. One of the best parts of a meal at a Mexican restaurant is those "oh so delicious" charro beans. Soft, spicy and tasty, they are even better the next day. At the push of a button and a 1 hour wait you will have the best charro beans ever! MAKES 4 PORTIONS (WITH SOME LEFT OVER FOR THE NEXT DAY)

1 pound dried pinto beans

4 cups chicken broth

6 cloves garlic

2 jalapeños, seeded

1 large onion, diced

1 pound smoked bacon, cut into ½ inch strips

1 (15 ounce) can diced tomatoes, drained

1 tablespoon ground cumin

2 tablespoons chili powder

2 dried chipotle peppers

Salt and pepper to taste

1 cup chopped fresh cilantro

1 Place all of the ingredients into the pressure cooker and bring to a boil. Place the lid on; seal and pressure-cook on high for 60 minutes. Remove the two chipotle peppers and season with salt and pepper and garnish with the cilantro before serving.

2 Alternatively, place all of the ingredients into a heavy based pan and bring to a boil. Simmer for about 1 ½–2 hours until the beans are tender.

POMEGRANATE MARGARITA GRANITA/SORBET

MAKES 10 PORTIONS

6 cups water

2 cup sugar

1 ⅓ cups fresh lime juice

¾ cup triple sec

¾ cup tequila

1 teaspoon lime zest

½ cup pomegranate twist mix (available at liquor stores or drinks supply stores)

1 Stir the water and sugar in heavy medium saucepan over medium heat until the sugar dissolves. Increase heat and bring to boil. Boil for two minutes. Pour into wide casserole dish. Mix in the lime juice, triple sec, tequila and lime zest.

2 Refrigerate until cold, about 2 hours. Then freeze until semi firm, whisking occasionally, for about 3 hours. Cover and freeze until solid, at least 6 hours or overnight. Using a fork, scrape the surface of the granita to form crystals. Scoop crystals into frozen glasses, drizzle over some ice cold pomegranate twist mix and serve granita immediately.

3 Rather than serving in glasses I prefer to serve mine in scooped out limes, though this recipe is so good on a summer's night that I often use individual scooped out watermelons instead... just joking!

» *Crawfish Stuffed Red Snapper, page 58*

KENTUCKY DERBY PARTY

One of the highlights of my eleven years at Buckingham Palace was catering Royal lunch at The Derby Stakes, a horse race held on the first Saturday of June at Epsom Downs and dating back to the early 1800's. It's one of Britain's greatest national sporting events and Her Majesty, a huge fan of horse racing, looks forward to it every year. We would arrive at the course early and prepare a delicious lunch in the Royal box for the Queen and her guests. Once served, the rest of the afternoon was free for us chefs to wander the racecourse and take a look at the fillies—both two and four legged.

When I moved to the USA I missed those horse racing events. Sure we have a racecourse in Dallas but it doesn't host grand events like Royal Ascot or The Derby Stakes back home. The only thing that comes close is the Kentucky Derby held annually in Louisville on the first Saturday in May. Known as "the fastest two minutes in sports," it attracts a similar crowd like the English Derby, dressed to the nines and ready to party.

I look forward to this event every year and as much as I wish I could be there, I simply can't. Instead I host my own Kentucky Derby Party inviting friends over who dress up for lunch and come to watch the races. Of course, I've replaced the obligatory Pimms Cup with a mint julep and my recipes are Southern inspired.

CRAWFISH STUFFED RED SNAPPER

I REMEMBER BEING IN DESTIN, FLORIDA WATCHING THE BOATS COMING IN WITH AMAZING RED SNAPPER. So fresh, it's eyes followed you around the quay side. I thought, how cool to take some of that snapper and create an amazing dish with shrimp and crawfish from the gulf. Well, here it is. Just the perfect thing for Kentucky Derby lunch. MAKES 4 PORTIONS

½ cup diced celery

½ cup diced red onion

½ cup diced red bell pepper

2 tablespoons olive oil

1 teaspoon minced garlic

1 pinch dried thyme

Salt and pepper to taste

½ cup grated Parmesan cheese

1 pinch cayenne pepper

¼ cup fresh chopped dill

4 (6 ounce) red snapper fillets, cut into equal halves

12 ounces fresh shrimp, 21/25 count, peeled and deveined

4 ounces crawfish tails, chopped

2 sticks unsalted butter, softened but not melted

1 In a large skillet, sauté the celery, onion and bell pepper in the olive oil until soft and translucent. Stir in the garlic, thyme parmesan and cayenne pepper.

2 Pulse the shrimp and crawfish in a food processor and add the softened butter. Season with salt and pepper. Add the peppers and onion mix and stir until combined. Place four pieces of aluminum foil (each large enough to fold into a packet) onto a cutting board with a piece of red snapper on top of each. Spoon a large tablespoon of shrimp mix on to each of the four pieces of the snapper and top with another piece of snapper. Add another spoon of shrimp mix. Fold the aluminum foil to wrap the fish parcels and bake at 350°F for about 10-15 minutes until the fish is cooked.

3 Remove the parcels from the oven and let rest for about 5-10 minutes. Open the parcels and place on a serving platter. Garnish with fresh chopped dill.

SOUTHERN CORNBREAD

SERVES 4-6 PEOPLE

¼ cup of oil, shortening or bacon fat

1-½ cups of all purpose white or yellow cornmeal

3 tablespoons of all purpose flour

1 teaspoon of baking soda

1 teaspoon of baking powder

1 teaspoon of kosher salt

2 cups of buttermilk, more or less

1 large egg, lightly beaten

1 Preheat oven to 450°F. Add the fat to a well seasoned 10-inch cast iron skillet and place the skillet into the oven to melt the fat and heat the skillet. In a bowl, whisk together the cornmeal, flour, baking soda, baking powder and salt. Using mitts, carefully remove the skillet from the oven and swirl the hot fat around to coat the entire skillet.

2 Pour the fat from the skillet into the cornmeal mixture; stir. Stir in half of the buttermilk and add the egg; add more buttermilk as needed to make a thick but pourable batter. Depending on the grind of your cornmeal and the type of buttermilk you use, you may not need it all. Fold ingredients and don't beat the batter. Pour the cornmeal mixture into the hot skillet. Carefully place directly into the oven and bake at 450°F for about 20 to 25 minutes. Remove the skillet from the oven, let rest for 5 minutes, the cut and serve.

SWEET COLESLAW

ONE THING I LEARNT WHEN MAKING COLESLAW IN TEXAS IS THAT THE SOUTHERNERS REALLY DO LIKE IT SWEET. Don't skimp on the sugar; in fact add a little more if you want to!
MAKES 4 PORTIONS

1 pound green cabbage, finely shredded

4 carrots, grated

1 medium sweet yellow onion, chopped

1 cup mayonnaise

¼ cup buttermilk

¼ cup Creole mustard

¾ cup granulated sugar

¼ teaspoon celery seeds

¼ cup apple cider vinegar

¼ teaspoon salt

1 teaspoon black pepper

1 Add the cabbage, carrots and onion to a large bowl. In a separate bowl, whisk together the mayonnaise, buttermilk, mustard, sugar, celery seeds and vinegar and season with salt and pepper. Stir the mayonnaise mix into the cabbage, onions and carrots and massage in. Refrigerate for at least an hour—overnight is even better.

SWEET POTATO CHEESECAKE WITH PECAN PRALINE TOPPING

MAKES 4 LARGE OR 8 THIN WEDGES

8 whole graham crackers, broken

½ cup pecans (2 ounces)

1 tablespoon light brown sugar

5 tablespoons unsalted butter, melted, plus more for greasing the pan

2 cups pureed sweet potatoes

1 ½ cups cream cheese (14 ounces), at room temperature

1 ½ cups granulated sugar

1 teaspoon salt

1 teaspoon cinnamon

¼ teaspoon freshly ground nutmeg

¼ teaspoon ground cloves

¼ teaspoon ground allspice

5 large eggs, at room temperature

1 cup heavy cream, at room temperature

1 tablespoon fresh lemon juice

2 teaspoons pure vanilla extract

1 Preheat the oven to 400°F. Butter the bottom and side of a 9-inch spring form pan. In a food processor, pulse the graham crackers, pecans and brown sugar until finely ground. Add the melted butter and pulse just until incorporated. Press the crumbs onto the bottom of the prepared pan. Bake the crust for about 8 minutes, until lightly browned and let cool completely.

2 In a standing electric mixer fitted with a bowl and paddle, beat the cream cheese until smooth. With the machine on, add the sugar with the salt, cinnamon, nutmeg, cloves and allspice to the cream cheese and beat until creamy. Add the sweet potato puree and beat in. Add the eggs one at a time, beating well and scraping down the bowl between each addition. Beat in the heavy cream, lemon juice and vanilla until the cheesecake mixture is smooth.

3 Pour the cheesecake mixture into the crust and bake for 12 minutes. Lower the oven temperature to 225°F and bake for about 3 hours, until an instant-read thermometer inserted in the center registers 150°F. Let the cheesecake cool on a rack, then cover and refrigerate overnight. When chilled, remove the ring and transfer the cake to a plate. Using a warm knife, cut the cake into wedges and serve with the Pecan Praline Topping and whipped cream.

PECAN PRALINE TOPPING

1 ½ sticks unsalted butter

¾ cup dark brown sugar

½ cup heavy cream

¼ teaspoon salt

2 cups pecans (8 ounces), lightly toasted and chopped

1 Preheat the oven to 350°F. In a large saucepan, combine the butter and brown sugar and cook over moderate heat, stirring, until smooth. Stir in the heavy cream and salt and bring to a boil. Simmer just until slightly thickened, about 3 minutes. Let the caramel cool. Fold in the chopped pecans.

SUMMER

After a whirlwind round of job interviews, I was headed back to the airport to catch a nonstop flight to London. With a few minutes to spare, I realized that I hadn't eaten anything since breakfast. I was starving. Luckily, this being Dallas, there was an airport outpost of a well-known local barbecue place (I no longer remember the name), and I decided to grab a sandwich before boarding. Brisket was on the menu, and it wasn't the tiny rolled brisket I was used to cooking at home for Sunday dinner. The chef behind the counter pulled out the biggest piece of meat I had ever seen and began carving thin slices and layering them onto lightly toasted white bread with a dab of extra bbq sauce on top, sliced in half and put in a Styrofoam container. I joked that I had never seen such a giant piece of meat, and he laconically responded, "You think so? I got twice this size in the back." Maybe true, maybe Texas-sized exaggeration.

The sandwich seemed utterly simple. Bread, sauce and meat ...lots of meat. No tomato, no lettuce, nothing extra. But it was a revelation. Tender, smoky meat with a hint of sweetness and soft yielding bread whose sole function was to make sure I didn't have to pick the meat up with my hands. This was something I had never tasted before. Still recognizably beef but pulled toward fire and smoke so deeply that it became something new. Happily I got a job offer and moved with my family to Plano, Texas, where for the past two decades we have enjoyed more barbecue than I can remember.

Texas, like a lot of southern states, is culinarily predisposed to cooking over an open flame. From eating and living here, I've learned a lot about grilling and smoking. My youngest, Harry, born in the States, can't imagine that barbecue doesn't exist everywhere, and in a way he is right. But while grilling over live coals is still a predominant form of cooking throughout much of the world, it is perhaps unique to the southern parts of America that the flavor of smoke from burning big chunks of Hickory and Mesquite wood is so deeply appreciated.

There is a lot of wonky literature out there about barbecuing and smoking meat, filled with arcane timetables, precise temperature settings, pitmaster's lore and a gender divide that puts men in charge of the grill. Now, while I can only speak to my experience in Texas, I'll go out on a limb and say that most of that barbecue mystique is utter nonsense. Men and women grill equally well and making a perfectly smoked brisket or side of ribs does not require a PhD. Still, the myth of Texas barbecue pulls deeply on people's psyche here. The countryside around Dallas is sprinkled

with lakes, and many people have cabins that are a source of lots of weekend partying. It was by being invited to lakefront parties over the years that I developed a theory that I call the "Zen of BBQ." This theory is that all the fussy rules about slowly smoking meat are just a front. The whole point of barbecue is sitting outside on a lazy afternoon and enjoying the view. It is about the kids shouting in the pool or jumping off the short pier into the lake. It is about sweet tea and beer and horseshoes. It is about gathering around the smoker for hours, relaxing, telling stories and "visiting." Great barbecued brisket, ribs and hot links aren't really the goal. They are the by-product (and a delicious one at that). Spending time with each other is the goal.

Recognizing that makes me nostalgic about summer vacations as a child. In the north of England, the summertime break lasts six weeks. That's it. And of those six weeks, you can be assured that only one includes sunshine. The rest is damp, drizzly and overcast. No matter. Like many working class families, mine would fill up the family camper and go caravaning to Skegness beach where the English Channel opens up to the North Sea or to Wales or Scotland or down into Cornwall for a proper look around.

We traveled around and did the English version of summertime outdoor eating—we picnicked. Mum would pack a hamper full of sandwiches (my favorite was chopped eggs with salad cream and mustard topped with watercress), some gorgeous butter, cold ham and cheeses, pork pies, sausage rolls, drinks and fruit, and we would eat impromptu outdoor meals wherever we found ourselves. We picnicked because Dad couldn't afford restaurant prices with the five of us and because it was more fun.

I remember the slow and unstructured pace of summer. If we were at Skegness, my siblings and I could play outdoors all day long at the beach, assured that dinner would be an amazing piece of fried fish so fresh I imagined it jumping from the sea, across the beach and into the pan in our caravan. A vacation highlight was always strawberry picking. Sitting outside with a bowl of fresh strawberries with whipped cream or real clotted cream is such a lovely childhood memory for me. Even our kids can't wait to go strawberry picking each time we go back to England in the summer.

As I grew older the lure of sunshine took me to Italy or Spain, where I could be found at the beach or trawling the outdoor food markets. Now in Texas we do a bit of the reverse: a little less sun and a lot less heat. So we may travel back to England or go to northern California or the East Coast like Massachusetts and Maine. Still we do spend a good bit of time in Dallas where the stove is unplugged for the summer and we exist on cold salads and anything we can toss on the grill or smoker.

By the time the sun dips down in the sky, the evening cools off a bit, and family and friends sit around enjoying a chilled cocktail. I'm usually manning the grill, anything from vegetable kebabs, grilled flatbreads or classic ribs and burgers. Someone always brings a salad or a case of local beer to try. My kids, all teenagers, seem to muster up an army of friends when I'm cooking. They come around to fill their plates with food and then migrate to their favorite spot in the garden to have their own important conversations. The evening unfolds so slowly that it isn't until we see each other by flickering votive candles that we realize how long we've been outside. Time for a bit of ice cream or a cold slice of watermelon to round out the evening. The sky is filled with stars, and it seems a shame to go inside. Maybe just another half hour...

» *Peach & Basil Pavlova, page 71*

POOLSIDE BRUNCH

R estaurant chefs can get quite opinionated when it comes to brunch. Anthony Bourdain, one of its most vocal critics, has trolled brunch as a "horrible, cynical way of unloading leftovers and charging three times as much as you ordinarily charge for breakfast."

While I don't disagree with him when it comes to eating brunch at a restaurant, I've got nothing but good things to say about inviting friends over to the house for brunch. Listen, if I can stay at home knocking about in shorts and a T-shirt, have time alone for a long contemplative cup of coffee and be creative and cook whatever I feel like, then it's a perfect day. Brunch checks all those boxes, and for that reason it has my eternal affection.

But I do have some rules. Rule #1 – Stop with the mimosas. No one needs to drink bad champagne early in the day. It's depressing. Instead ditch the alcohol for some top quality brewed coffee and freshly squeezed juice plus a pitcher of iced water with cucumber and lemons sliced into it. Rule #2 – Don't call lunch "brunch." I've been invited to "brunches" that don't start until noon which is ridiculously late. Really, if you are going to have brunch, get things going by 10:30 AM. That allows guests to have a good visit and still get on with the rest of their day. Rule #3 – Remember, room temperature food is your friend. When the weather is hot, I'm much more likely to put out a few salads, some cold fruit or a cold soup, and something fast from the grill. Summer heat means finicky appetites and I want guests to eat at their leisure.

There's no rush. The kids are in the pool having fun, the adults are having a good caffeine fueled chat, and there is plenty of food is on hand to keep everyone sated until dinner.

LOBSTER, LUMP CRAB & HEIRLOOM TOMATO SALAD

THIS SALAD IS TAILOR MADE FOR GUESTS. The lobster and crab make it a bit luxurious, the tomatoes and asparagus go beautifully together, and the herbal dressing brings out the best of both the seafood and veggies. Easy to assemble in advance and dress at the last minute, this salad looks gorgeous on the plate and tastes amazing. Splurge on the freshest lobster and crab and get a few perfectly ripe tomatoes from the farmer's market. It will make all the difference. SERVES 4

PURÈED HERB DRESSING

2 cups mixed fresh herbs of dill, chives, basil, tarragon, parsley in equal parts or as preferred

6 tablespoons white balsamic vinegar

6 tablespoons extra virgin olive oil

2 tablespoons onions, chopped

1 tablespoon granulated sugar

FOR THE SALAD

1 small cooked lobster, meat removed and cut into bite size pieces

8 ounces jumbo lump crabmeat, picked over for any bits of shell

2 pounds ripe heirloom tomatoes cut into bite size pieces

1 small bunch asparagus tips, steamed until tender

¼ cup finely chopped red onion

1 tablespoon champagne vinegar

2 tablespoons extra virgin olive oil

2 cups mixed salad leaves

Salt and pepper, to taste

1 An hour before serving, blend all of the ingredients for the herb dressing until smooth. Adjust seasoning, adding salt and pepper to taste. This dressing can also be refrigerated for up to three days.

2 Combine the tomatoes, asparagus, red onion, vinegar and oil. Stir in the crab meat and lobster and season with salt and pepper.

3 Divide the salad leaves between the plates and top with the lobster, crab and tomato salad. Drizzle with the herb dressing just before serving.

» *Lobster, Lumb Crab & Heirloom Tomato Salad, page 68*

YELLOW TOMATO & WATERMELON GAZPACHO

FEEL FREE TO FIDDLE WITH THE VINEGAR, WORCESTERSHIRE AND CUMIN SEASONINGS, BUT DON'T LEAVE THEM OUT COMPLETELY. They provide a needed complexity and flavor punch with each cool sip. I like to serve these in small glasses for easy drinking. MAKES 4 PORTIONS

1 ½ pound yellow tomatoes

1 cup watermelon, peeled, seeded and chopped

½ cup chopped yellow bell pepper

½ cup chopped onion

1 small jalapeño, seeded and minced

1 medium garlic clove, minced

¼ cup extra-virgin olive oil

1 lime, juiced

2 teaspoons white balsamic vinegar

2 teaspoons Worcestershire sauce

½ teaspoon toasted, ground cumin

1 teaspoon kosher salt

¼ teaspoon freshly ground black pepper

2 tablespoons fresh mint leaves, cut into very thin strips

1 Place the tomatoes into a large mixing bowl. Add the watermelon, bell pepper, onion, jalapeño, garlic clove, olive oil, lime juice, white balsamic vinegar, Worcestershire sauce, cumin, salt and pepper and stir to combine.

2 Transfer the mixture to a blender and puree for 15 to 20 seconds on high speed until smooth. Cover and chill for 2 hours and up to overnight. Garnish with the fresh mint.

PEACH & BASIL PAVLOVA

PAVLOVA'S ARE PERFECT FOR SUMMER—A LIGHT MERINGUE TOPPED WITH PLENTY OF FRESH FRUIT AND WHIPPED CREAM.

8 egg whites

2 cups granulated sugar

¼ cup cornstarch

2 teaspoons white wine vinegar

1 teaspoon vanilla

2 cups heavy cream, whipped stiff

2 tablespoons chopped basil

6 peaches, stoned and cut into bite size pieces

2 large baking sheets

2 large sheets parchment paper

1 Preheat the oven to 250°F.

2 Whip the egg whites until stiff using an electric mixer. Gradually whisk in the sugar and then the cornstarch, vinegar and vanilla to make the meringue.

3 Place the parchment paper onto the baking sheets and divide the meringue mix between the two making two neat 9 inch circles the same size.

4 Bake at 250°F for about three hours. Remove from the oven and allow to cool completely before moving off the baking sheet.

5 Place one disc of meringue onto a large serving platter and carefully spoon and spread half of the whipped cream over the top. Do the same with half of the peaches and half of the basil. Place the second disc on top and repeat the process using the remaining peaches, basil and cream. Serve immediately.

» *Chocolate Marquis, page 77*

GRADUATION CELEBRATION

It's hard to say whether graduations are more for the graduate or the graduate's parents! But to be sure everyone is just beaming with happiness. Our school district is large with nearly 750 kids per grade, so there are lots of students and crowds of family and extended family out in force to celebrate. As soon as the final student crosses the stage, there is a cheer from the crowd and everyone agrees it is time to get out of their seats and start to party.

The following menu can be doubled, tripled or quadrupled easily to accommodate a crowd at the house. Best of all, dessert and salad can be made ahead and the chicken and asparagus all prepped for their final cooking. This meal tastes good hot and at room temperature so you can feed kids (yours and assorted others) as they stop by for a few minutes before heading out to the next party! Better yet, it's a menu that won't break the bank and that's good news, because you are going to need every penny soon...

HEIRLOOM TOMATO BASIL & BURRATA SALAD

I MAKE NO EXCUSES FOR PUTTING THIS "GLORIFIED CAPRESE SALAD" RECIPE IN THE BOOK. In the summer I have an abundance of heirloom tomatoes in my garden and this becomes our family salad, often several days in a row. To really experience this joy of nature, you have to pick the tomatoes along with some mixed salad leaves and basil just before you start making the salad. Slice the tomatoes really thin and fan them around a large platter. Sprinkle with English Maldon sea salt and fresh ground pepper and place a burrata or two in the center of the plate. Watch with joy as family and friends spoon into the burrata and the Stracciatella cream runs over the tomatoes. MAKES 4 PORTIONS

4 large heirloom tomatoes (try to get different types and colors)

2 large burrata

4 cups salad leaves

1 tablespoon shredded basil

2 tablespoons extra virgin olive oil

1 tablespoon white balsamic vinegar

English Maldon (or any good finishing salt) to taste

Fresh ground black pepper

1 Slice the tomatoes all the same thickness and fan around a serving platter. Place the two burratas in the center of the plates. Toss the salad leaves and shredded basil on top of the tomatoes.

2 Drizzle with the olive oil and white balsamic. Finish with the salt and pepper just before serving.

PARMESAN-PANKO CRUSTED CHICKEN WITH LEMON BUTTER SAUCE

FOR THE CHICKEN

4 boneless, skinless chicken breasts, flattened to ½" thickness

1 cup buttermilk

1 tablespoon olive oil

1 egg, beaten and mixed with 1 clove minced garlic and ¼ stick melted butter

¼ cup flour

1 cup Panko

⅓ cup grated Parmesan cheese

2 tablespoons chopped fresh chives

¼ cup finely chopped green onions

FOR THE SAUCE

3 tablespoons butter

2 tablespoons olive oil

1 small onion, finely diced

2 tablespoons flour

1 chicken bouillon cube

½ cup dry white wine

1 cup water

½ teaspoon Worcestershire sauce

½ cup heavy cream

1 Soak the chicken breast in the buttermilk for at least 2 hours or overnight.

2 Preheat the oven to 400°F. Dredge the chicken in the flour, then the egg mix and then the panko. Season with salt and pepper and sauté on one side in the oil. Turn the chicken over and divide the Parmesan between the tops of each piece of chicken. If you are making this for a crowd, lightly brown the chicken in a sauté pan and transfer to a large baking sheet. Then top with parmesan. Sprinkle the chives on top. Bake for about 8 minutes.

3 In a large pan, melt the butter and oil and add the onion and cook until soft. Stir in the flour, broth cube, white wine, water, Worcestershire sauce and cream and reduce. Season with salt and pepper. Keep the sauce warm while the chicken is cooking.

4 Lay the cooked chicken onto a serving plate, spoon the sauce over the top before serving and garnish with chopped green onions.

GRILLED ASPARAGUS WITH BACON & REDUCED BALSAMIC

THIS RECIPE CALLS FOR REDUCED BALSAMIC VINEGAR WHICH YOU CAN PURCHASE IN ANY GOOD FOODS STORE. But it is also easy to make; just use regular balsamic vinegar and boil it until it has reduced by two-thirds, is syrupy and coats the back of a spoon. MAKES 4 PORTIONS

2 large bunches thick asparagus

4 slices center cut smoked bacon

1 tablespoon olive oil

1 tablespoon reduced balsamic vinegar

Salt and pepper to taste

1 Heat the grill to medium high.

2 Snap the asparagus two thirds down from the tips and discard the smaller end pieces. These would be too woody to cook.

3 Wrap about five pieces of asparagus in a slice of bacon and place onto a baking sheet. Repeat the process with the rest of the asparagus and bacon.

4 Drizzle the oil over the bacon/asparagus rolls and place on the grill for about 6-8 minutes, turning them from time to time, until the bacon is cooked and asparagus is easily pierced with a knife.

5 Remove to a serving plate, season with salt and pepper if needed and drizzle over the reduced balsamic just before serving.

CHOCOLATE MARQUIS

THIS IS A CHOCOHOLICS DREAM WITH DARK CHOCOLATE, BUTTER, SUGAR AND COCOA POWDER. A slice goes a long way, especially when you gild it with a drizzle of caramel sauce.

YIELDS 4 TO 6 SLICES

1 ¼ cups 60% dark chocolate

½ cup unsalted butter

½ cup granulated sugar, divided

2 tablespoons cocoa powder

3 egg yolks

2 tablespoons brandy

1 ¼ cups heavy cream

Caramel Sauce (see recipe below)

1 Melt the chocolate in a large bowl over hot water and set aside to cool. Cream together half of the sugar with all of the butter with an electric mixer until light and fluffy then add in the cocoa powder and mix together until combined and smooth.

2 In a separate bowl, whisk the yolks with the remaining sugar until pale in color then add the brandy and mix in.

3 In a third bowl, whip the heavy cream until it forms soft peaks. Add the chocolate to the butter/sugar mixture and fold in. Now fold in the egg yolk/sugar mixture followed by the whipped cream.

4 Spoon into a plastic wrap lined decorative mold or 1 pound loaf tin also lined with plastic wrap. Cover the top with plastic wrap as well. Freeze the mix at least three hours or overnight. Remove from the mold carefully and slice. Drizzle with caramel sauce or serve separately.

CARAMEL SAUCE

MAKES 4 PORTIONS

½ cup granulated sugar

¼ cup water

¾ cup + 1 tablespoon of heavy cream, at room temperature

½ stick unsalted butter (2 ounces) at room temperature

Pinch of salt

1 In a saucepan, bring the sugar and water to a boil. Cook until it turns a deep amber color, stopping before it begins to burn. Carefully and with your face at a distance from the pot, stir in half of the cream. It will bubble up furiously. Remove the caramel from the heat and stir in the remaining cream, butter and salt and keep whisking it to form a smooth sauce. Allow to cool.

FIRE UP THE GRILL

I've learned a lot about grilling since I've been in the States. We do grill food in Britain, but not all that often, and our weather rarely cooperates. I've been to too many "barbecues" where everyone is indoors watching the poor host outside manning the grill with one hand and holding an umbrella with the other. I think that is why the concept of barbecue in the UK is more often than not limited to sausages, burgers and chicken drumsticks. If anyone dared to put a whole brisket on the grill, they might endure four seasons of weather just waiting for it to cook!

But here in the States, I learned just how creative and flexible grilling is; an expansive cooking technique that includes direct fire cooking, offset cooking, smoking, pit cooking and even baking. I've seen pizza stones heated directly on the grill for pizza night, which makes good sense since many simple propane fired grills can heat up to 700°F, giving you that lovely, slightly charred pizza crust.

I had fun with this menu, using the grill for each course through dessert. There is grilled chicken on a bed of grilled veggie quinoa and quickly grilled hangar steak on bruschetta with white beans and touch of blue cheese. To finish the evening off, there is grilled bananas topped with luscious crème anglaise and toffee sauce. I do make sure to give the grill a good scrape down between courses, and I recommend you invest in an inexpensive wire brush. You can also place a sheet of aluminum on the grill between courses and close the lid. Anything on the grates will turn to ash, and you simply brush it away. After all, you dont want your bananas to taste like chicken.

MINUTE STEAKS WITH BLUE CHEESE & CARAMELIZED ONIONS & CANNELLINI BRUSCHETTA

BEEF AND BLUE CHEESE ARE A BELOVED MCGRADY FAMILY COMBINATION. These minute steaks are easy to pull together, are great at room temperature and satisfy a hungry bunch of teens and adults. Oh, and they go great with beer!

While bruschetta (and please pronounce it as brusk-etta. It drives me nuts in restaurants when they say brush–etta) are normally served as an open faced bite, these are more like sandwiches, the better to hold together the beef with the arugula and caramelized onions. MAKES 4 PORTIONS

FOR THE ONIONS
½ red onion, peeled and sliced thin

1 teaspoon sugar

2 tablespoons olive oil

FOR THE CANNELLINI SPREAD
1 (11 ounce) can of cannellini beans, drained and rinsed

2 cloves garlic, minced

½ cup extra virgin olive oil

1 teaspoon fresh rosemary, chopped

Zest of 1 lemon

4 (3 ounce) center cut beef tenderloin steaks, flattened to ½ inch thick

Salt, pepper, garlic powder, English mustard powder to season

2 tablespoons olive oil, for steaks

1 small clove garlic, minced

2 tablespoons extra virgin olive oil

8 slices crusty white bread

¼ cup Maytag blue cheese crumbles

1 cup fresh arugula

1 Prepare the cannellini spread. In a food processor, blend all of the ingredients together and season with salt and pepper. Set aside.

2 Caramelize the onions. In a heavy based pan, add the oil and onions and cook on low until they start to soften, add the sugar and salt to taste and stir until the onions start to turn brown. This can take up to 20 minutes, so be patient. Set aside and keep warm.

3 Preheat the grill to around 400°F. Brush each steak front and back with the oil and sprinkle each with the salt, pepper, garlic and mustard.

Place on the grill over direct heat for about 30 seconds and then turn over and repeat. Remove to a plate to rest.

4 Stir the minced garlic into the olive oil and brush each slice of bread top and bottom. Place on the grill to heat, crust and get grill marks. Turn the bread over and do the other side. Season with salt.

5 Spread some cannellini paste onto four slices of the bruschetta. Lay one of the steaks on top of one. Top with the onions and some maytag cheese crumbles and arugula and place the second piece of bruschetta on top.

» *Minute Steaks with Blue Cheese & Caramelized Onions & Cannellini Bruschetta, page 80*

CHILI & GARLIC CHICKEN SKEWERS WITH GRILLED VEGETABLE QUINOA

THIS IS REALLY A FULL MEAL, WITH PROTEIN, HEALTHY CARBS AND FRESH VEGETABLES. You can easily double or triple the recipe. MAKES 4 PORTIONS

1 pound boneless, skinless chicken breast or thighs, cut into 16 small chunks

16 baby mushrooms

16 cherry tomatoes

1 teaspoon chili and garlic sauce

1 teaspoon Chinese five spice powder

1 tablespoon extra virgin olive oil

1 lime, juice and zest

¼ cup chopped fresh cilantro

4 twelve inch skewers

1 cup quinoa

2 cups water

½ medium red onion, peeled and sliced, root on

1 red bell pepper, seeds removed and sliced long-ways

1 zucchini, top and tailed and sliced long-ways into three

2 sticks celery, cut into half, long-ways

½ head fennel, sliced ½ inch thick

¼ cup extra virgin olive oil

Salt and pepper

¼ cup white balsamic vinegar

¼ cup extra virgin olive oil

1 teaspoon Dijon mustard

1 teaspoon granulated sugar

Salt and pepper

¼ cup finely chopped green onions

1 In a large bowl add the chili and garlic sauce, five spice, olive oil, lime juice and zest. Stir in the chicken and marinade for at least 10 minutes. Thread 4 pieces of chicken with four mushrooms and four cherry tomatoes onto each skewer, place on a clean plate and refrigerate.

2 In a large pan add the quinoa and cold water and bring to the boil over high heat, reduce to a simmer and cover with a lid. Cook until the liquid has all absorbed. Remove from the heat, remove the lid and allow to cool.

3 Heat the grill to medium high and brush the vegetables with the olive oil. Sprinkle with the salt and cook on the grill for about 6 minutes or until soft. Remove to a cutting board and chop into bite size pieces. Place the skewers on the grill and cook for 2 minutes per side.

4 Blend the vinegar, olive oil, sugar, salt and pepper and mustard until combined. Stir the dressing into the quinoa, season with salt and pepper and add the vegetables. Sprinkle the green onions over the top of the quinoa. Lay the cooked chicken skewers on top of the quinoa.

GRILLED BANANAS WITH VANILLA CRÈME ANGLAISE & TOFFEE SAUCE

MAKES 4 PORTIONS

4 large firm bananas, skin on

4 small sheets aluminum foil

FOR THE TOFFEE SAUCE

½ cup unsalted butter

½ cup light brown sugar

¼ cup corn syrup

¾ cup heavy cream

FOR THE VANILLA CRÈME ANGLAISE

1 cup milk

3 egg yolks

Vanilla bean extract

2 tablespoons granulated sugar

¼ cup heavy cream

1 Prepare the toffee sauce. Heat the butter, brown sugar, corn syrup on high, stirring all the time until the sugar has dissolved. Boil for three minutes, remove from the heat, and then carefully whisk in the cream. If the mix is not smooth, return it to the stove and stir until it becomes smooth.

2 Prepare the crème anglaise. Bring the milk to a boil in a heavy based pot. Whisk the egg yolks, vanilla and sugar until combined. Pour the boiling milk on to the egg mix and whisk until smooth. Return the mix to the pot and place back on the heat. Stir until the mix has the consistency of heavy cream.

3 Remove the mix from the heat and whisk in the cream. Refrigerate for at least an hour before serving.

4 Preheat the grill to medium high. Wrap the bananas individually in the aluminum foil but not completely, leaving one side with the banana peel exposed. This exposed peel you then pierce lengthwise, making a cut about half inch deep. This allows steam to escape from the roasted banana. Place the bananas on the grill, foil side down and grill for about 10 minutes.

5 Remove to serving plates, discard the aluminum and serve with the toffee and crème anglaise sauces.

INGREDIENT
SPOTLIGHT

Dry Rubs, Wet Rubs & Marinades

There is a lot of talk about rubs and marinades as great ways to add flavor to your grilled foods. But it does lead to a lot of confusion. When should you marinate and when should you rely on a rub?

MARINADES

The biggest difference between marinades and rubs is that marinades typically include acid such as lemon or lime juice, vinegar, shredded papaya or alcohol which works to break down meat's connective tissue and make it tender. How long you marinate meat depends on the kind of meat. If you are cooking a protein that is already tender—fish, chicken breast or beef filet—marinate briefly, no more than 2 hours (and in the case of fish, even less time may be sufficient—30 minutes can be plenty). Tougher cuts of meat should marinate from 4 hours to overnight. Don't leave your meat marinating for longer than that or the texture will be mushy.

Remember:

- Place meat and marinade in a large, resealable plastic bag or a glass or ceramic bowl with plastic wrap on top. Metal bowls can interact with the acid and impart an off flavor.
- Marinate food in the fridge. Meat sitting on the counter for too long, even with an acidic marinade, can start growing bacteria and can cause food poisoning.
- Any leftover marinade in the bag or bowl can be used to baste the meat while it's on the grill, up until the last 10 minutes of cooking. No matter how tasty it is, do not use leftover marinade as a sauce—it's contaminated by the raw meat. If you really want to re-use it, boil it for about 3 minutes.
- Use approximately ¼ cup of marinade for each pound of meat.

RUBS

Rubs are mixes of spices and seasoning that add flavor but don't tenderize. Dry rubs are just what they sound like, a collection of dry seasonings that make a powdery mix. A wet rub will have the same dry ingredients with the addition of oil, sugar, mustard or even soy sauce to make a kind of spreadable paste. Salt is a key component to both dry and wet rubs, and salt tends to initially draw out moisture from a protein. However, if you leave the dry rub on longer, the meat will begin to reabsorb the moisture and take all the flavorings with it inside the muscle. Rubs, both wet and dry, also create an exterior rim of flavor around the protein.

Just like it sounds, rubs are meant to be rubbed onto your meat. To get the best results, make sure your protein is patted dry before you give it a good coating. I like to use dry rubs for seafood, fish, lamb chops and pork tenderloins, or a premium cut of steak that doesn't need to be tenderized. Dry rubs are also great for fatty cuts of meat like pork shoulder or butt, short ribs or anything that will cook slowly but have enough fat to literally self-baste.

Wet rubs are good for grilling meat or vegetables that might need a bit more moisture. I like to use wet rubs for things like Tri Tip, flank, veggie kebabs and even potato hobo packs. Wet rubs can also be used in slow cooking for baby back ribs and chicken drumsticks.

In Texas it seems that rubs are more popular for barbecuing and grilling than marinades. Certainly every grill master seems to have a "special recipe" held as a close family secret. Well, I am more than happy to share my rub recipe with you, and I think you will really like it.

MY BBQ RUB

1 cup coarse kosher salt

½ cup coarse black pepper

¼ cup smoked paprika

¼ cup dry English mustard powder

¼ cup ancho chili powder

¼ cup garlic powder

¼ cup dried thyme

½ cup soft brown sugar

Mix all of the ingredients together and store in an airtight container.
It will stay fresh for several months.

» *Caramelized Onion & Brie Burgers, page 89*

FOURTH OF JULY FIREWORKS FIESTA

Most older English are rather ambivalent about Independence Day, which they often view as just another flag waving opportunity for the Americans, while younger Brits born after 1990 always think it has something to do with aliens and and the actor Will Smith. Even the British who live here find it a somewhat discomfiting show of patriotism. Such outward enthusiasm goes totally against the grain. But ask them how they feel about burgers on the grill, beer and fireworks and most will nod and say, "Well, that's lovely." Yes it is.

I'm sure there are places where a vegetarian Fourth of July feast is perfectly acceptable (I'm looking at you California), but here in Texas meat is always on the menu, the more varieties the better. From the Parma ham in the cantaloupe salad, to the burgers and ribs, meat makes an appearance everywhere in this menu, except the blueberry and strawberry dessert. Of course you can serve some of the cantaloupe sans ham and tuck one or two veggie burgers on the grill to make everyone happy. And isn't that what Fourth of July should be? A day we all celebrate, each in our own different way, together.

CANTALOUPE SALAD WITH PARMA HAM, MINT, LIME & GINGER

I DON'T THINK YOU WILL FIND AN EASIER OR TASTIER RECIPE THAN THIS IN ANY COOKBOOK. It's a few simple ingredients coming together to create a salad symphony. This dish has "summer" written all over it. MAKES 4 PORTIONS

1 whole cantaloupe

8 slices Prosciutto ham

1 tablespoon fresh chopped mint

1 small lime, zest and juice

1 teaspoon fresh crushed ginger

1 tablespoon reduced balsamic glaze, see note below

2 cups baby arugula

1 Peel and remove the seeds from the melon. Cut into thin wedges and arrange in a line on a serving platter. Sprinkle with the ginger, mint and lime zest and juice and layer the Prosciutto over the melon to cover it. Pile the arugula on top of the ham and drizzle with the reduced balsamic just before serving.

Note: Balsamic glaze can either be purchased at any good foods store or made by reducing balsamic vinegar by two-thirds; i.e. to make one tablespoon of glaze start with three tablespoons of balsamic vinegar.

CARAMELIZED ONION & BRIE BURGERS

THESE ARE TEXAS SIZED STUFFED BURGERS, CLOCKING IN AT 8 OUNCES OF BEEF EACH. I'm not a burger purist here, so please feel free to make substitutions with a different cheeses or smaller patties. Even more heretical, I like to season my meat a bit before it goes on the grill. I think you should try it and tell me what you think! MAKES 4 PORTIONS

FOR THE ONIONS

2 tablespoons olive oil

1 red onion, halved and thinly sliced

Pinch of sugar

Salt and pepper

2 pounds ground beef

1 teaspoon salt

1 teaspoon black pepper

½ teaspoon garlic powder

½ teaspoon English mustard powder

⅛ teaspoon celery seeds

4 ounces Brie cheese, cut into small pieces

½ cup fresh cilantro

1 clove garlic

¼ cup olive oil

2 tablespoons white balsamic vinegar

Salt and pepper to taste

4 cups baby arugula, or less if you are putting it on top of the burger in the bun

1 Heat your grill to high. Heat the 2 tablespoons olive oil in a sauté pan over medium heat; add the red onions, sugar and salt. Cook until soft and caramelized stirring occasionally. Remove to a plate to cool.

2 In a large mixing bowl, add the beef, salt, pepper, garlic powder, mustard and celery seeds and mix until combined. Divide the mix into eight equal burger patties.

3 Top four of the patties with the Brie and onion in the center of each patty and lay the other four patties on top and carefully sealing the beef around the edges so the Brie doesn't leak.

4 Grill the burgers for about 5 minutes each side for a rare burger, longer for medium or well done. While the burgers are cooking blend the cilantro, garlic, olive oil, balsamic vinegar in a blender and season with salt and pepper and set aside.

5 Serve the burgers in burger buns or plated with arugula and drizzle the cilantro dressing over the leaves before serving.

OVEN BAKED BABY BACK RIBS

MAKES 4 PORTIONS

2 racks baby back ribs, about 2 pounds each

2 tablespoons Instant espresso powder

½ cup brown sugar

2 tablespoons Chipotle chili powder

1 tablespoon cocoa powder

1 tablespoon coarse salt

1 tablespoon dried oregano

2 teaspoons black pepper

1 cup apple juice

1 Preheat the oven to 300°F.

2 Remove the silvery membrane from the concave back of the ribs by pulling carefully with paper towel or ask your butcher to do it before you purchase the ribs. Mix together the espresso powder, brown sugar, chili powder, cocoa powder, salt, oregano and black pepper.

3 Place the ribs on a large, foil-lined baking sheet and coat with the rub front and back. Bake the ribs in the oven (uncovered) for about 2 hours.

4 Remove from the oven and turn the ribs onto the other side, cover with the apple juice and cover with aluminum foil. Cook for another hour until the ribs are fork tender and pull apart from the bone.

WHITE CHOCOLATE, BLUEBERRY & STRAWBERRY CROUSTADE

PEOPLE I MEET OFTEN INSIST THAT "I CAN'T DO PASTRY, I DON'T HAVE COLD HANDS." I'm not sure if this is a myth or not, but many people would rather buy a ready-made pastry shell than make one themselves. To be honest, I think it has more to do with rolling the pastry out and lining tart pans. This recipe uses phyllo dough and is super easy to make. You have to be gentle though when it comes to putting the fruit in so it doesn't collapse. Well worth the effort, this delicious red, white and blue dessert really will wow your family and friends.

TIP: always let the dough thaw in the refrigerator overnight. This will keep the sheets whole when it's time to unroll them. As you unroll the sheets, place a damp towel over the remaining phyllo so it doesn't dry out and start to break apart.

1 eight inch loose bottom tart pan	**¾ cup white chocolate chips, about six ounces**	**2 cups fresh strawberries, hulled and quartered**
12 sheets phyllo pastry	**½ cup heavy whipping cream (at room temperature)**	**2 cups fresh blueberries**
½ cup unsalted butter, melted	**1 egg white**	**¼ cup powdered sugar**
1 egg yolk		

1 Preheat the oven to 400°F.

2 Unroll the phyllo dough sheets and cut in half. Lay one sheet inside the pan and allow it to come up the sides. Mix the melted butter with the egg yolk and using a pastry brush lightly brush the pastry sheet. Place the second sheet on top at a different angle creating a nice overlay. Repeat the process, circling around the pan, with all of the sheets. Scrunch up the extra phyllo on the sides and tease it into the pan creating a well in the bottom for the filling once baked.

3 Bake the pastry shell for about 15-20 minutes until golden brown. Remove from the oven to cool completely.

4 Prepare the chocolate filling. Melt the chocolate in a large bowl set over a pan of simmering water. When melted, remove the bowl and set aside to cool. In a separate bowl, whip the egg white until stiff. Set aside.

5 In a third bowl, whip the heavy cream into soft peaks. Fold the whipped cream into the cooled melted chocolate and then fold in the stiff whipped egg white. Pour the mix into the center of the pastry shell and refrigerate for at least 3 hours, until nicely set. Garnish the top with the berries and dust the outer shell of the pastry shell with powdered sugar just before serving.

» *Chicken Tikka Masala Pizza, page 96*

GARDEN PIZZA PARTY

Pizza has come a long way from its southern Italian roots to be one of the most beloved dishes around the world. I've had pizza, good pizza, almost everywhere I have traveled, including throughout Asia and into Northern Europe. Evidently Indians in New Delhi are absolutely mad for pizza, and China, a country not known for its cheese or cheese eating habits, opens a new Pizza Hut store every single day. I think pizza's enormous popularity has to do with the fact that it presents a blank canvas, adaptable to any number of cuisines and tastes. Even more wonderful is that the best pizzeria can be right in your kitchen.

I really enjoy making pizza at home, and I have a lot of fun with my children and their friends as we try new and wonderful combinations. One friend had visited Norway, where he found out that pizza isn't pizza without lots of paprika and ham. Another let me know that a proper Korean pizza has pepperoni, bulgogi, pickles and a good smear of gochuchang chile paste. My own children seem to like a fusion approach to pizza, and over time we have come up with a few delicious family favorites, forgoing the usual cheese and pepperoni. There is a classic fig, Parma ham and goat cheese pizza which I could eat every day when fresh figs are in season. It is delicious. Come fall a slightly Frenchified galette of squash, apple and blue cheese tastes terrific. Something spicier is the old Indo-British favorite, chicken tikka masala, but reconceived as a pizza topping with a nice dollop of cilantro chutney and a drizzle of cooling yogurt. Even a simple store bought flatbread can be turned into a Thai(ish) pizza with a bit of red curry sauce and chicken.

As long as you have all your ingredients ready at hand, becoming the household pizzaiolo isn't all that hard. It's just shape, top, bake, cut, serve. Then repeat.

RUSTIC FIG PROSCIUTTO & GOAT CHEESE PIZZA

MAKES 1 LARGE PIZZA

PIZZA CRUST
1 package fast active dry yeast

1 teaspoon granulated sugar

1 cup warm water

3 cups bread flour

½ teaspoon salt

2 tablespoons olive oil

FOR THE TOPPING
1 ½ cups fresh goat cheese

½ red onion, sliced thin

6 ripe fresh figs

8 thin slices prosciutto

2 tablespoons extra virgin olive oil

2 cups baby arugula

⅓ cup balsamic vinegar reduced to a tablespoon

1 Prepare the pizza dough. Dissolve the yeast and sugar in lukewarm water. Add the flour, salt and oil and mix together to form a dough. Place somewhere warm, covered until the dough has doubled in size. Knock the dough back again and knead into a pliable ball. Roll out the dough to make one large 12" round pizza.

2 Crumble the goat cheese onto the dough. Top with the red onion, figs and prosciutto. Drizzle the olive oil on top. Bake at 400°F for 10-12 minutes.

3 Remove from the oven and place the arugula on top of the pizza. Drizzle with the balsamic vinegar and serve.

SQUASH & APPLE GALETTES WITH BLUE CHEESE

THIS GALETTE IS A CROSS BETWEEN A PIZZA AND A TART. The pastry crust does call for a combination of butter and lard which will make it taste great and be somewhat more pliable than an all butter crust. Paired with a tangle of salad greens, this is a meal all in itself.

MAKES 4 PORTIONS

1 ¼ cups all purpose flour

¼ teaspoon salt

¼ cup cold unsalted butter, diced

¼ cup lard, diced

1 egg + 1-2 tablespoons of cold water if necessary

1 small butternut squash cut into bite size cubes

1 red onion, sliced fine

¼ cup canola oil

1 large Granny Smith apple peeled and cut into thin slices

½ cup Maytag blue cheese, crumbled

1 Mix the flour, salt and butter in a food processor to make fine crumbs. Add the egg and mix until it forms a dough. Refrigerate for at least 1 hour.

2 Preheat the oven to 400°F. Toss the squash and red onion in the rapeseed oil and tip onto a baking sheet. Bake for about 20 minutes or until fork tender.

3 Roll out the dough on a lightly floured surface into a 12-inch circle. Place the dough on a baking sheet and place the cooked squash, red onion and apple on the dough, leaving at least an inch free around the edge.

4 Fold over the edges of the dough and bake until the crust is brown and the apples, squash, and onions are soft, about 45 minutes. Sprinkle the blue cheese over the filling and bake for a further 5 minutes. Cut the galette into wedges and serve.

CHICKEN TIKKA MASALA PIZZA

THIS IS ALWAYS A SURPRISE DISH FOR GUESTS WHO NEVER CONNECT INDIAN FLAVORS WITH PIZZA. In fact, while I'm taking a slight liberty with the word "pizza" here, there is absolutely nothing unusual about chicken tikka being scooped up with pieces of naan and popped into the mouth. I love the chewy quality of naan bread, and there are some good frozen versions on supermarket shelves these days. That makes life all the easier. The recipe below is for four naan bread pizzas, but naan sizes may vary where you live. Just keep making them until you are all out of bread or chicken tikka masala, whichever comes first. MAKES 4 PORTIONS

4 boneless skinless chicken breasts, about 1 ½ pounds

3 tablespoons toasted ground cumin

3 tablespoons paprika

2 tablespoons ground coriander seed

2 teaspoons ground turmeric

1 teaspoon cayenne pepper

6 cloves garlic, crushed

1 tablespoon fresh ginger, grated

2 cups plain yogurt

¼ cup lime juice

½ teaspoon kosher salt

4 tablespoons butter

1 large onion, thinly sliced

1 (14 ounce) can diced tomatoes

½ cup roughly chopped cilantro

½ cup heavy cream

4 store bought naan breads

1   Heat oven to 350°F. Mix together the cumin, paprika, coriander, turmeric and cayenne pepper in a large bowl. Add the garlic, ginger, yogurt, lime juice, salt and whisk to combine. Add the chicken breasts and massage the rub into the chicken. Refrigerate for a few hours or overnight.

2   Remove the chicken from the marinade and place onto a baking sheet. Keep the marinade and set aside. Bake the chicken for about 8-10 minutes until just tender.

3   Melt the butter in a heavy based pan and add the onions and a pinch of salt. Cook on a low heat until they begin to soften. Add the tomatoes and heavy cream. Then add the marinade the chicken was in. Simmer for at least 20 minutes. Adjust the seasoning with salt and pepper. Once you have the consistency of a thick sauce remove from the stove and allow to cool.

4   Slice the chicken breasts into bite size pieces and stir into the sauce. Divide the chicken and sauce between the four Naan breads and bake at 400°F for about 8-10 minutes. Sprinkle the cilantro on top of each just before serving.

THAI CHICKEN & RED CURRY FLATBREAD

OK, THIS ONE REALLY IS A CULTURAL MASHUP, BUT IT TASTES SO GOOD! Take a classic flatbread dough, top it with Thai curry chicken, some veggies, chopped peanuts and cilantro and finish with generous layer of shredded mozzarella. Each bite is spicy, sweet, crunchy and gooey. Should I even bother to mention how good it is with beer? You probably already guessed that.

MAKES 4 PORTIONS

THE MARINADE
2 chicken breast, boneless, skinless, about 1 lb.

2 tablespoons red curry paste

¼ cup fresh lime juice

2 teaspoons fresh ginger, crushed

1 clove garlic, crushed

1 tablespoon vegetable oil

½ teaspoon salt

THE FLATBREAD
1 package active yeast

½ teaspoon sugar

1 ¾ cup bread flour

1 teaspoon salt

¾ to 1 cup water

1 teaspoon olive oil

THE TOPPING
½ cup green onions finely sliced

½ cup grated carrots

1 red bell pepper, diced

½ cup salted peanuts

1 cup bean sprouts

1 cup fresh rough chopped cilantro

1 whole large mozzarella, thinly sliced

1 In a large bowl add the curry paste, lime juice, ginger, garlic and vegetable oil. Mix well. Add the chicken, salt and coat well with the paste. Refrigerate for at least 4 hours or overnight.

2 In a large mixing bowl or in an electric mixer with a dough hook, combine the yeast, sugar, flour and salt. Slowly mix in the water and oil until the dough begins to form a ball. Knead until the dough is smooth and elastic. Place dough in bowl, and cover with a damp cloth. Place in a warm area to double in size. This will take about 1 hour.

3 Once the dough has doubled, knock the dough back and cut into half. Freeze half of the dough for another time and with the remaining dough break into 4 pieces and roll out to make 8-10 inch flat bread rectangles. Either in an ungreased hot skillet or on the grill, cook the dough for about 2 minutes each side, until just slightly done. Set aside each grilled flatbread on a rack to cool.

4 Heat the oven to 350°F. Remove the chicken from the marinade, season it with salt and pepper and bake the chicken about 10-15 minutes depending upon the thickness of the breast. Let the chicken cool slightly and then cut it into bite size pieces and divide between the four flat breads. Top each with the green onions, carrots, bell pepper, peanuts, bean sprouts and cilantro finishing with the mozzarella. Transfer the flatbreads to a baking sheet and bake for about 6-8 minutes until the cheese melts and the toppings are warmed through.

COCKTAILS & FUN(D)RAISING

Every so often you find yourself hosting a big event. It could be a local school fundraiser or a larger philanthropic annual event like an auction. Dallas, where I live, is terrifically philanthropic, and I both participate in and cater to lots of events. Each year it seems the American palate becomes both more diverse and more adventurous. You do need to have some of the standards—I don't think cold poached shrimp with a spicy horseradish and tomato sauce will ever go out of style. But a cocktail party can now include lamb kofta, sushi, black-eyed pea falafel with yogurt sauce, spoonfuls of spicy Mexican ceviche, and even tiny lasagna "muffins."

If you are going to host a big event, you will need help. So by all means give an "all hands on deck" shout out to the PTA parents' or develop a formal budget with the charity you hope to raise funds for, including money for rentals of tables, chairs, decorations, music, waitstaff, kitchen helpers and even valet parking. The bigger the event, the more time spent organizing it all, and to help, I've laid out some entertaining tips in the last section of this book.

But don't forget that doing good should be fun! When the day arrives and the first guests pull up to the house, it is officially go time. Get the food on out of the kitchen, have the music pumping and the cocktails flowing. Time to party!

LAMB KOFTAS

THIS RECIPE CAN BE DOUBLED AND TRIPLED EASILY, AND IT DOESN'T MATTER HOW MANY YOU MAKE, THEY WILL BE ALL EATEN BY EVENING'S END. Its success relies on that not so secret catering truth—everyone loves a meatball. Especially a wonderfully seasoned meatball served with a cooling mint raita. MAKES 16 AS APPETIZERS

Soak 16 bamboo skewers in water for about an hour

1 pound ground lamb

½ medium onion, very finely diced

2 cloves garlic, minced

¼ cup fresh mint, chopped

¼ cup fresh cilantro, chopped

2 teaspoons lemon zest, grated

2 teaspoons lemon juice

1 ½ teaspoons cumin

1 egg whites

Salt and black pepper to taste

1   Combine all of the ingredients together in a large bowl until well blended and smooth.

2   Wet hands lightly, divide mixture into 16 equal portions and form into uniform cylinder shapes. Thread each cylinder onto a damp bamboo skewer and set on a baking sheet. Cover with plastic wrap and refrigerate several hours or overnight.

3   Remove from the refrigerator and place skewers on a hot, lightly oiled grill over high heat and grill for about 6-8 minutes, turning until nicely browned and cooked through. Koftas can also be cooked in a 400°F oven. Sear on all sides first in a large frying pan and then bake for about 6-8 minutes. Serve with mint raita.

MINT RAITA

MAKES ABOUT 2 CUPS

1 (7 ounce) Greek yogurt

1 teaspoon cumin

2 tablespoons fresh mint, chopped

Juice of 1 lemon

½ teaspoon salt

1 clove garlic, crushed

½ an English cucumber, peeled, seeds removed and finely chopped

1   In a large bowl combine all of the above ingredients. Adjust seasoning and refrigerate.

SPINACH, MUSHROOM & ARTICHOKE CASSEROLE

MAKES 4 PORTIONS

2 (10 ounce) packets frozen chopped spinach

2 tablespoons olive oil

4 tablespoons butter

1 onion, finely chopped

1 small packet of mushrooms, sliced

⅓ cup flour

2 cups chicken broth

1 can artichoke bottoms, drained and quartered

½ cup parmesan cheese, grated

1 cup cheddar cheese, grated

½ cup panko or breadcrumbs

¼ cup Stilton cheese

3 slices Pancetta, torn and fried to crisp

Salt and pepper to taste

1 Preheat the oven to 350°F and grease an 8x8x2 casserole dish

2 Thaw the bag of spinach in warm water. When thawed, open the bag and squeeze out excess water from spinach.

3 In a heavy based pan, melt the butter and olive oil over high heat and add the onion and sliced mushrooms. Add a little salt, reduce the heat to medium and stir until the onions start to soften, about 3 minutes.

4 Stir in the flour and gradually incorporate the chicken broth. Simmer for 5 minutes and season the sauce with the salt and pepper.

5 Lay half of the spinach and half of the artichokes on the bottom of the casserole dish. Pour ½ of the mushroom sauce on top and sprinkle with ½ of the parmesan and ½ of the cheddar. Place the remaining spinach and artichokes on top, add the remaining sauce. Top with the remaining cheddar and parmesan and sprinkle the breadcrumbs or panko over the top of the cheeses. Crumble the Stilton cheese into walnut size pieces and dot around the top of the dish and top with the Pancetta.

6 Bake in the center of the oven until the sauce is bubbling and the top golden brown, about 30 minutes. Serve with crackers or flatbreads to scoop.

THAI RED CURRY SCOTCH EGGS WITH SWEET CHILI SAUCE

TRUST AN ENGLISHMAN TO REWORK THE SCOTCH EGG IN EVERY POSSIBLE WAY. MAKES 4 EGGS

4 large eggs, hard boiled and shelled

8 ounces ground pork

1 tablespoon Thai red curry paste

¼ cup fresh cilantro, finely chopped

Salt and freshly ground white pepper

½ cup flour, seasoned with salt and freshly ground black pepper

2 eggs, beaten with 2 tablespoons milk

1 cup panko or dried breadcrumbs

1 cup peanuts, finely chopped (optional)

Vegetable oil, for deep frying

4 tablespoons chopped cilantro

FOR THE CHILI SAUCE

3 tablespoons chili paste

2 teaspoons minced garlic

½ cup rice wine vinegar

⅔ cup water

⅔ cup sugar

1 teaspoon salt

4 teaspoons cornstarch

1 Mix the ground pork with the Thai red curry paste and cilantro in a bowl and season with salt and white pepper. Divide into 4.

2 Dry each egg with paper towel and then wrap the sausage meat around each egg. Make sure the coating is smooth and completely covers the egg. Place in the refrigerator to firm up for 10 minutes.

3 Prepare a crumbing station by adding flour to a wide bowl. In another bowl beat the two eggs with milk. On a large plate combine the peanuts with the breadcrumbs. Roll each one first in the flour, then in the beaten egg, making sure it is completely coated. Then finally roll in the breadcrumbs/peanuts to completely cover.

4 Preheat the oven to 350°F. Heat the pan of oil to 350°F. Carefully place each Scotch egg into the hot oil and deep-fry until golden and crisp, remove to a roasting pan and place in the oven until the pork coating on the eggs is completely cooked through. To serve, cut each egg into four quarters and arrange on a tray. Drizzle the chili sauce over top and garnish with chopped cilantro. Serve hot.

5 **FOR THE CHILI SAUCE** Combine everything in a small sauce pan and mix. Once blended, bring to a boil, reduce heat and simmer about 5 minutes.

BLUE CHEESE SHORTBREAD CANAPÉS WITH GOAT CHEESE & FIGS

THE SHORTBREADS CAN BE MADE IN ADVANCE, COOLED COMPLETELY AND THEN FROZEN. Just thaw, top and serve. MAKES ABOUT 30 CANAPÉS

½ cup butter, at room temperature

1 cup crumbled blue cheese

1 cup all-purpose flour

Pinch of cayenne pepper

Pinch of salt

½ cup soft goat cheese

4 fresh ripe figs cut into small wedges

1　In a food processor add the butter, blue cheese, flour, cayenne and salt and pulse until blended. Shape into a log, wrap in parchment or plastic wrap and refrigerate until firm or freeze for up to 3 months.

2　To bake, slice ¼-inch thick and bake on an ungreased baking sheet at 350°F for 10 minutes, or until pale golden around the edges.

3　Allow the shortbread to cool and top with a little goat cheese and a piece of fig.

» *White Chocolate & Rhubarb Créme Brulee with Clotted Cream Shortbread, page 109*

LUNCH FOR A LAZY SUNDAY AFTERNOON

Sunday Lunch is a treasured English tradition, a pause in all the busyness of life. The classic image is of an impossibly large roast of beef or lamb being carved at the table surrounded by Yorkshire puddings, a variety of vegetable dishes and a gravy boat filled to the rim. It might start any time between 1 PM and 3 PM, smack in the middle of the day, and it unspools leisurely over hours. Sunday lunch is defiantly anti-modern and unhurried, a conscious refusal of the status quo, and, to my mind, utterly brilliant.

If you are inviting friends over, you've got to apply some criteria. Generally (and of course, you can do what you wish) pub friends are preferred to hiking friends, chatty friends are better than reticent ones and fine connoisseurs of weekends will always edge out workaholics. A friend just back from exotic travels? Yes, you make the list too.

Since it is summertime, I'll not be pulling a leg of lamb out of the oven. Instead we will have some easy grilled steak, mashed potatoes with lots of cream and butter (because who on earth doesn't like mashed potatoes?) and vegetable kebabs. I've got my favorite white chocolate crème brulee with a little stewed rhubarb chilling in the fridge for dessert. Add to that one or two bottles of wine I've been meaning to open and, should things go as planned, a nice bottle of scotch to sip later. The world will continue to spin and people will be rushing about doing all sorts of amazing things, and I will be just fine, sitting here with the people I love who have all turned their phones to silent.

SOY GINGER GARLIC HANGER STEAKS

HANGER STEAKS ARE WITHOUT A DOUBT THE CHEF'S FAVORITE CUT OF MEAT. Whenever I have chef friends over to grill outdoors, I always buy hanger steaks. Less than half the price of other steaks but double the flavor. No need to add salt in this recipe; the soy sauce will do that for you. MAKES 4 PORTIONS

3 tablespoons brown sugar

½ cup lite soy sauce

2 tablespoons vegetable oil + extra for grilling

3 tablespoons sesame oil

1 tablespoon crushed fresh ginger

3 cloves fresh garlic, crushed

1 tablespoon chili garlic paste

2 spring onions, chopped

½ teaspoon of toasted sesame seeds

2 pounds hanger steak

1 In a large bowl whisk together the brown sugar, soy sauce, vegetable oil, sesame oil, ginger, garlic and chili garlic paste until combined. Place the hanger steaks in a large ziplock bag and pour the marinade into the bag. Massage into the meat and then refrigerate for at least 4 hours or overnight.

2 Remove the steaks from the fridge at least an hour before cooking to allow them to come to room temperature. Preheat a gas or charcoal grill until medium-hot.

3 Lightly brush the grill with vegetable oil. Remove the steaks from the bag and discard the marinade. Grill the steak for about 6 minutes in total (for medium rare) turning them once halfway through cooking.

4 Transfer steaks to a chopping board and leave to rest for about 5 minutes. Thinly slice the steak against the grain and garnish with the spring onions and sesame seeds to serve.

SESAME VEGETABLE KEBABS

MAKES 4 PORTIONS

¼ cup lime juice

4 garlic cloves, minced

¼ cup soy sauce

2 tablespoons sesame oil

1 ½ tablespoons crushed fresh ginger

2 teaspoons chili garlic sauce

1 pound medium fresh baby mushrooms, cleaned

1 pound cherry tomatoes

2 zucchini cut into 1-inch pieces

1 large sweet yellow pepper, cut into 1-inch pieces

1 small red onion, cut into wedges

Wooden skewers, soaked for at least an hour in cold water

1   Whisk together in a large bowl the lime juice, garlic, soy sauce, sesame oil, chili garlic sauce and ginger. Add the mushrooms, tomatoes, pepper, zucchini and onion to a ziplock bag and pour in the marinade. Refrigerate for at least 1 hour. Drain and reserve marinade.

2   Thread the vegetables onto the soaked wooden skewers. Grill over medium heat for about 6-8 minutes or until tender, basting frequently with reserved marinade and turning once. Serve the skewers alongside the hangar steak.

WASABI MASHED POTATOES

NOTE: A little wasabi goes a long way... MAKES 4 PORTIONS

2 pounds russet potatoes, about 4 large potatoes

½ cup heavy cream

1 cup freshly grated Parmesan cheese

4 tablespoons unsalted butter, softened

1 teaspoon (or to taste) wasabi paste

1 teaspoon salt

¼ cup finely sliced green onions

1 Peel the potatoes and cut them into 1-inch chunks. Place into a large pot and cover with cold water. Bring potatoes to a boil and cook until fork tender, 15-20 minutes. Drain the potatoes and return to the pot. Mash with a potato masher until there are no lumps.

2 Add the cream and butter and stir into the potatoes. Stir in the Parmesan cheese, wasabi and salt and adjust the seasoning. Spoon into a serving dish and top with the green onions.

WHITE CHOCOLATE & RHUBARB CRÈME BRULEE WITH CLOTTED CREAM SHORTBREAD

MAKES 4 PORTIONS

THE BRULEE
6 egg yolks

½ cup sugar

1 teaspoon vanilla paste or extract

2 cups heavy cream

2 ounces white chocolate, grated

1 tablespoon Cointreau

Sugar for glazing

THE RHUBARB
1 pound fresh rhubarb

1 cup light brown sugar

THE SHORTBREAD
½ cup flour

¼ cup powdered sugar

¼ cup cornstarch

½ cup unsalted butter

1 jar clotted cream, or ½ cup heavy whipped cream, or 8 ounces of mascarpone

1 Preheat the oven to 350°F.

2 Prepare the brulee. Whisk the yolks, sugar and vanilla together in a large bowl until combined. Set aside. Bring the cream to a boil in a heavy bottomed saucepan. When the cream is hot, whisk it very slowly into the egg mixture, to warm and temper the eggs. Return the egg/cream mixture to the pan and over a low heat stir the brulee mix until it starts to thicken. Remove the saucepan from the heat and stir in the white chocolate. Remove 1 cup of the mixture from the pan, stir in the 1 tablespoon Cointreau and refrigerate. Pour the remaining mix into an earthenware dish and bake until set, about 20 minutes. The center of the brulee needs to look like "set jello" when lightly shaken. Allow to cool and refrigerate. Sprinkle with the sugar and glaze with a brulee torch or under the broiler, until golden brown.

3 Place the rhubarb and sugar in a small pan and stir. Place on a low heat and simmer until the rhubarb is just tender and easily pierced with a fork. Remove from the heat and refrigerate.

4 For the shortbread, rub the flour, cornstarch, butter and powdered sugar together in a large bowl to form a dough. Roll out and cut into cookies. Place on a baking sheet and bake for about 10 minutes until the edges start to brown. Allow to cool.

5 In a sundae dish build the dessert. Spoon layers of brulee, rhubarb and the Cointreau cream. Place one of the shortbread cookies on top and garnish with the clotted cream.

FALL

September in Texas can be a beast. Hot and humid with oppressive swollen skies. Air conditioners running full blast just so you can stay dry. Children trudging home from school wilting under their heavy backpacks. By contrast, there is truly nothing as wonderful as a golden English September, so soft and lovely that its memory can sustain you as the wet chill of fall descends and settles deep into your bones, where it will stay lodged until spring. By October we English begin the annual rites of "putting on the kettle," constantly heating up cups of tea to stay warm.

For years after I moved to Texas, I could never remember if my extended family visited us in the spring or fall. In my mind it was always summer. After all, wasn't it hot and weren't we grilling out in the backyard? But over the years, I've begun to notice more subtle changes. The afternoon light slants lower across the kitchen counters, and the mornings are just a touch cooler. The languor of summer heat begins to lift.

There is something too about the school calendar that even now makes me think that September really starts a new year. It's supposed to be January, but to be honest, I'm more interested in taking stock of the upcoming year in September. Fall is a busy time. There are end of summer events, followed by school activities, Halloween tricks and treats, Thanksgiving celebrations and the mad sprint to Christmas. There is so much to look forward to and experience. I silently promise myself that this year I'm going to... brush up on my Spanish, make time to coach soccer, immerse myself in some new cooking techniques, etc... But mostly I'll map out my upcoming year and set goals, culinary and personal.

Fall entertaining bridges the casual, "drop in anytime" feeling of summer with the more intimate dinner parties of winter evenings. We'll open the house during early fall for family barbeques with loads of kids shrieking around the garden and pitchers of sangria for the grownups. There are still plenty of tomatoes, pepper and summer squash coming in from the garden to enjoy perfumed with the potted basil's last leaves. Melons, big and small, are soft and filled with juice. The final corn crop from a nearby farm is being harvested, and the deluge of fresh plucked ears is sweet and inexpensive. We eat a lot of it.

But soon I'll roll the grill into storage and start roasting again. Entertaining may still be casual outdoor buffets, but now we'll need votive candles and light cardigans for later in the evening. My ever organized wife begins to plan out our fall calendar including parties, school fundraisers, quick trips, and guest lists for Thanksgiving. I, on the other hand, look forward to carving pumpkins—something I never did as a kid—and enjoying all things ghostly and ghastly. As the cooler weather draws in, I turn to slow cooked braises. Nothing beats buttoning up to walk the dog for an hour than returning to the smell of Guinness braised pork shanks with apples and prunes wafting through the house and one of the kids shouting, "Dad! How long will dinner be?"

Our local farmers markets are filled with onions, leeks, new potatoes, hard squashes, root vegetables and greens, greens, greens. I love to cook them all. At our house a pan of vegetables roasting alongside a pork loin or standing rib roast in the oven and a great bottle (or two) of wine have been at the heart of some of our most memorable get togethers. The holidays are right around the corner, and the wine has everyone feeling just a bit festive. Cheers.

FARMERS MAR

VEGGIES FROM THE FARMER'S MARKET

Our local farmer's market is held in the high school parking lot on Saturday mornings and by 8 AM there is a long line of impatient drivers trying to get a prime parking spot. Not everyone has had their coffee (including me), and there are more than a few grumpy shoppers (again, guilty). But at a farmer's market I am like a kid in a toy store. Getting my hands on gorgeous local apples or better yet, late season ripe figs, mellows my mood and just makes me happier. If you don't regularly check out your local farmer's market, I'm here to encourage you to do so. The vendors are happy to be there, you will run into a neighbor who has some juicy gossip (and who doesn't like that?), and the produce for sale is worthy of the fine brush of a French impressionist painter. It is really a beautiful sight, and I always end up buying too much.

So what to do with all those beautiful vegetables? There are soups to be made, salads, platters of roasted vegetables or just sliced up and munched raw for snacking. The list is long. In this menu I've included a delicious fall take on bruschetta and a warm vegetable salad that is flexible enough to take advantage of the all the perfectly ripe veggies you find at the market. I think these are the perfect kinds of dishes to feed a family or serve to a friend, proving definitively that you don't need meat at the center of the plate for every meal. There is a growing "meatless Monday" movement across the United States, and I, a true meat lover, know that vegetables keep me and those I love happy and healthy. I can support that.

BAKED FIG & GOAT CHEESE BRUSCHETTA WITH CHERRY FENNEL COMPOTE

MAKES 4 PORTIONS

FOR THE BRUSCHETTA
1 loaf ciabatta bread, cut into eight 1-inch slices

¼ cup olive oil

2 cloves garlic, minced

1 pinch salt

1 pinch pepper

8 ripe figs, sliced

8 slices Prosciutto

½ cup goat cheese, crumbled

FOR THE CHERRY FENNEL COMPOTE
1 cup fresh cherries, pitted and halved

1 teaspoon fennel seeds

¼ cup sugar

1 teaspoon lemon juice

1 Preheat the oven to 350°F.

2 Mix the olive oil with the garlic, salt and pepper in a small bowl and brush onto each side of the bread. Place on a baking sheet and bake for about 10 minutes then turn the bread over and bake another 5 minutes. Remove from the oven and set aside.

3 **FOR THE COMPOTE** In a small skillet heat the fennel seeds for about 3 minutes to release the oils in the seeds. Add the sugar, cherries and lemon juice and stir. Simmer for about 10 minutes until the cherries soften and become pulpy. Set aside to cool.

4 Lay out the slices of Prosciutto onto a small cookie sheet or a wide sauté pan. Divide the goat cheese and place a mound in the center of each slice of Prosciutto. Place one whole fig, sliced and fanned out slightly, on top of the goat cheese leaving enough room to be able to fold the edges of the prosciutto over the fig. Place on a baking sheet and bake in the center of the oven for about 10 minutes or until the goat cheese has melted.

5 Place a teaspoon of the cherry fennel compote onto each of the bread slices. Remove the wrapped figs from the oven and carefully lay one on each of the bread. Serve immediately.

WARM SALAD OF HONEY ROAST PARSNIPS, CRANBERRIES, PEARS & MACADAMIA NUTS WITH A CREAMY GORGONZOLA DRESSING

MAKES 4 PORTIONS

4 small parsnips, peeled and quartered lengthways

2 tablespoons olive oil

1 tablespoon honey

Salt and pepper to taste

4 handfuls of arugula leaves, washed

2 ripe dessert pears, peeled and cut into wedges

¼ cup dried cranberries

¼ cup macadamia nuts, lightly toasted

FOR THE DRESSING

6 ounces Gorgonzola cheese, rind removed

3 tablespoons white wine vinegar

¼ cup olive oil

Black pepper

1 Preheat the oven to 400°F.

2 Place the parsnips in a roasting pan and coat with the olive oil. Drizzle with the honey and season to taste. Roast in the preheated oven for about 20 minutes, until golden. Remove from the oven and leave in a warm place.

3 To make the dressing, mash the Gorgonzola in a mixing bowl. Stir in the wine vinegar, then add the olive oil and seasoning and whisk until the mixture is fairly smooth. Season with salt and pepper.

4 Arrange the arugula on four serving plates and top with the pears, cranberries, nuts and parsnips. Pour over the dressing and serve.

RUSTIC DATE & APPLE PASTRY

THIS DESSERT IS FORMED AS A GALETTE, WHICH IS JUST A FANCY FRENCH COOKING TERM FOR "ROUND." In this case, you don't put the pastry dough in a pie or tart tin. Just roll it out, fill the center with fruit and then fold over the pastry edges on to the fruit and brush the pastry with a little egg wash. SERVES 6

FOR THE PASTRY
¼ cup unsalted butter

¼ cup lard or solid vegetable shortening

1 ⅓ cups all purpose flour

Pinch of salt

½ teaspoon sugar

3 tablespoons cold water

½ teaspoon apple cider vinegar

FOR THE FILLING
3 tablespoons butter

3 pounds Granny Smith apples (about 6-8), peeled, cored, quartered and sliced

1 teaspoon ground cardamom

1 teaspoon cinnamon

⅓ cup honey

⅔ cup chopped walnuts

8 large Medjool dates, pitted and roughly chopped

1 large egg

2 tablespoons milk

3 tablespoons demerara sugar

FOR GARNISH
1 cup chilled whipping cream

1 teaspoon cinnamon

1 teaspoon vanilla paste or extract

2 tablespoons sugar

1 In a large bowl rub the butter and lard/shortening into the flour, sugar and salt until mixture resembles coarse meal. Add the water and vinegar and mix until moist clumps form, adding more water by teaspoonfuls if dough is dry. Gather dough into ball; flatten into disk. Wrap in plastic and refrigerate at least 30 minutes.

2 Melt the butter in a large skillet. Add the apples and sauté until they start to soften—about 10 minutes. Add the cardamom and cinnamon and ⅓ cup of the honey, stir in and cook 1 minute. Take it off the stove and allow to cool to lukewarm.

3 Preheat an oven to 350°F. Roll out dough to about a 12-inch round and place on a baking sheet. Spoon half of apple mixture over crust, leaving 2-inch plain border. Sprinkle dates and nuts over the apples. Top with remaining apple mixture. Fold outer edge of crust over apples (dough is delicate; press together any tears). Whisk egg and milk in bowl. Brush edges generously with egg mixture. Sprinkle the crust with the demerara sugar.

4 Bake until crust is golden brown, about 35 minutes. Cool for about 45 minutes. Whip the cream with the sugar, cinnamon and vanilla until stiff and serve with the pastry.

» *Rustic Date & Apple Pastry, page 118*

TECHNIQUE
SPOTLIGHT

Sous Vide Cooking at Home

Chefs like to say that there are no new recipes, just tweaks to old ones. Well that is not completely true. In fact, we create new recipes when we find new ingredients that were either overlooked or unknown. Consider the tomato in the fifteenth century and the acai berry ten years ago: new ingredients that created entirely new dishes. The same is true for new cooking techniques. Every chef learns early in their training that it is technique, not recipes, which are the cornerstone blocks of cuisine. How to boil properly, sauté properly, braise, grill, fry, steam, smoke, etc... You learn the technique and then you apply that technique across all sorts of ingredients.

One of the most recent technique to be embraced by chefs is sous vide. It's French for "under vacuum" and it originated in France in the mid-1970's when two chefs, Georges Pralus and Bruno Goussault, used water baths to cook food. It was Goussault who eventually developed the method on an industrial scale and introduced sous vide as a technique for professional chefs. Now, this idea is only slightly new. Preserving and cooking food in sealed packages is an ancient technique. Food can be cooked and covered in fat (confit), cooked in sealed jars, salted, dried, or, my favorite, cooked inside an animal bladder—hats off to you, Scotland! People have long known that protecting fresh food from the air can slow down its decay or stop it from drying out.

Sous vide cooking is easier than its fancy name might suggest. You simply place the ingredients into a plastic bag, remove the air using a vacuum sealer machine that also seals the bag. Then the bag is placed into a water bath set exactly at a target temperature. When the food reaches your target temperature you remove the bag from the water, take out the meat or fish, dry it with a paper towel and then give it a quick sear or other finish and serve it. But here's the thing: the defining feature of the sous vide method is not the elimination of air; it is accurate temperature control. A computer-controlled heater can warm a water bath to any temperature you set, and it can keep it there for hours, if needed.

By controlling temperature so closely, sous vide cooking can yield results that are nearly impossible to achieve by other cooking techniques. For example, a perfectly medium rare steak achieves an internal temperature of 139°F. In sous vide cooking you can place your sealed steak into a 139 degree water bath and in one hour the steak's internal temperature matches that of the water bath. Now, you have several options. Remove the steak from the water bath, give a quick turn on the grill and serve, or decide to keep the steak in the water bath for up to an additional three hours with no change in its internal temperature. For restaurateurs, sous vide effectively frees the chef from incessantly worrying about the time.

The steak is perfect now and will continue to be perfect and ready to serve for hours to come.

Same is true for salmon, one of my favorite dishes to cook via the sous vide technique. A perfectly cooked salmon, still moist and slightly pink in the center, is done at 123°F, a mere thirty minutes in a sous vide bath. You can then serve it right away or hold the fish for up to an additional three hours. This is a boon to chefs for whom perfectly cooked fish is typically achieved within a very tight time frame. Plus your sous vide fish (or beef or poultry) will be cooked evenly throughout. There are no dry edges to your salmon or shrinkage due to evaporation. That salmon on your plate is just as big as when you purchased it. A final benefit to sous vide cooking is that the closed bag effectively braises food, so ingredients cooked this way are often juicier and more tender.

So that dinner guest who just texted you that they are stuck in traffic and will be 30 minutes late? Relax and have another drink. Dinner is still going to be perfect.

» *Burgundy, Balsamic Beef Tenderloin, page 124,
and Bubble & Squeak, page 125*

A PROPER
SUNDAY DINNER

Y̱ou can take the Englishman out of England, but... well, you know the rest. For the English, a proper Sunday dinner is, at this point, almost a genetic trait. I still love it and miss my mother's Sunday dinners and my Nans too. Sunday dinner, or "Sunday roast" as it's called across the pond dates back to before WWII. Friday was payday and take away night—fish and chips for everyone! Saturday was shopping day, so dinner was often cold sliced meats and salad. Sunday was a roast. It might be a rolled shoulder of lamb, a bone in prime rib of beef, chicken, or a leg of pork. Anything left over was used the rest of the week, beef reappearing as Cottage Pie and potatoes and cabbage reheated in beef drippings to make Bubble & Squeak. Chicken got pulled off the bone to make an English curry.

My mother and father both came from large families. Seven heads in each. And my Nan loved to cook and was good at it. As the years passed and her children grew and left, my Nan would still cook a four pound chicken every Sunday. Often she would still be eating it come Thursday. When I asked her about it, she explained, "I have always cooked a Sunday roast. When your mum and her brothers and sister left home I told them that no matter where they were, on Sunday there would always be a chicken on the table and they would always be welcome." It was a tradition she continued without fail, until she could no longer. They say food smells bring back memories. I remember my Nan and her generosity every time I have a chicken roasting in the oven.

While my own children have grown up in the States and our mealtimes are sometimes squashed (or downright flattened) between sports, music lessons and schoolwork, I do insist that once a week they act like proper English children and sit down to dinner with their parents over a lovely roast and actual conversation. They all know that at Mom and Dad's, there will always be a proper Sunday dinner on the table with plenty for everyone. No need to call ahead!

BURGUNDY, BALSAMIC BEEF TENDERLOIN

I'M CONVINCED THIS TENDERLOIN RECIPE WILL MAKE YOU AN IMMEDIATE CONVERT TO SOUS VIDE COOKING. Below I've given you instructions for roasting the beef in the traditional manner and cooking it via sousvide. (Of course, you will need a sous-vide machine). You decide. SERVES 6

3 pounds beef tenderloin, trimmed of fat and silver skin

1 bottle Burgundy wine

1 cup balsamic vinegar

4 bay leaves

6 cloves of garlic, crushed

6 sprigs fresh thyme

1 extra large ziplock bag

1 tablespoon olive oil

FOR THE SAUCE

1 tablespoon olive oil

1 medium onion, chopped

2 stalks celery, chopped

1 small carrot, peeled and chopped

2 slices bacon, chopped

3 teaspoons flour

1-2 teaspoons of "Better than bouillon" (chicken base)

¼ cup tomato puree

½ cup chopped chives

1 In a large zip lock bag, place the tenderloin, wine, vinegar, bay leaves, garlic and thyme. Seal and refrigerate for up to 24 hours.

2 **PREPARE THE SAUCE** In a large pan add the olive oil, onion, celery, carrot and bacon. Sauté until the vegetables start to soften and the bacon gets a little brown. Stir in the flour and tomato puree and let cook for a minute. Remove the tenderloin from its marinade and set it aside. Add all the reserved marinade (including all the flavoring herbs and garlic) to the sautéed vegetables and bring to a boil, reduce the sauce by half. Add "Better than bouillon," whisk in to sauce and taste for seasoning. Strain the sauce through a sieve and discard the vegetables. Season with salt and pepper if needed and set it aside to keep warm.

3 **Sous Vide Method:** Set the sous vide waterbath to 139°F. Season the tenderloin with salt and pepper well, place it in a polyethylene plastic bag and vacuum seal. When the water bath reaches 139°F, place the tenderloin in the bath and set the timer for one hour. You may leave the beef in the sous vide machine for up to 4 hours without it overcooking or spoiling. Remove the tenderloin from the plastic bag, dry with paper towel, rub it with olive oil and quickly sear the tenderloin on top of the stove, or under a broiler, watching it carefully so it doesn't burn. Slice and serve with the warmed burgundy balsamic sauce.

4 **Traditional Method:** Dry the tenderloin with paper towel; rub the olive oil over the tenderloin and season with salt and pepper. Grill the tenderloin to desired doneness or sear in a large frying pan and roast at 400°F for about 35 minutes or desired doneness.

5 Let the meat rest for 15 minutes before slicing and spooning the sauce over. Garnish with the chopped chives.

BUBBLE & SQUEAK

3 pounds large red potatoes

1 pound cabbage

1 cup smoked bacon, about 5 ounces

½ teaspoon caraway seeds (optional)

Salt and pepper

2 tablespoons vegetable oil

1 Peel and quarter the potatoes. Put potatoes into a saucepan. Add ½ teaspoon salt. Add water until potatoes are covered. Bring to boil, reduce heat and simmer, covered, 15-20 minutes, or until done—a fork can easily be poked through them. Strain the water off the potatoes and mash them. Add salt and pepper to taste and set aside to cool.

2 Cut the cabbage in half and remove and discard the root. Cut the cabbage into small chunks and place in a pan of boiling water. Add ½ teaspoon of salt and cook until the cabbage is tender. Strain off the water and place the cabbage in cold water to refresh it. Strain off the water and set the cabbage aside.

3 Cut the bacon into ½ inch strips and place over high heat in a heavy based frying pan. Stir until the bacon is crispy and remove it to a paper towel and set aside, leave the bacon grease in the pan. Remove the pan from the heat and set aside for a moment. Now in a large bowl combine the potatoes, bacon and cabbage, stir in the caraway seeds and salt and pepper to taste.

4 Place the pan of bacon grease back on the heat and when medium hot, add half of the potato/cabbage mixture, pat down to about 2 inches thick and cook until the potato/cabbage mix starts to brown on the bottom. Using a spatula flip the potatoes over and brown the other side and remove from the pan when hot and crispy. Repeat with remaining potato/cabbage mix. Serve straight away.

CREAMED LEEKS WITH STILTON & PANCETTA

MAKES 4 PORTIONS

3 large leeks, white and light green only (about 1 pound when trimmed)

½ stick butter, 2 ounces

¼ cup flour

¼ cup cream

¼ cup chicken broth

1 tablespoon horseradish

Salt and pepper to taste

½ cup panko or breadcrumbs

2 ounces Stilton cheese, crumbled

1 tablespoon butter

2 slices Pancetta, torn into bite size pieces and deep fried until crisp

6 cup casserole dish

1 Preheat the oven to 350°F.

2 Peel the outer leaves off the leeks and trim off the dark green pieces. Cut ¾ of the way through each leek lengthways and then finely shred into about ⅛ inch pieces. Place the leeks in a large bowl, cover with cold water and agitate several times. Leave in the water for about 10 minutes. Leeks can be quite sandy and all that grit should fall to the bottom of the bowl. Drain and rewash making sure the water is clear and your leeks are totally clean.

3 In a large pan over high heat, melt the ½ stick of butter. Lift the leeks out of the water by hand and lightly squeezing them, drop them into the butter. Stir and add salt and pepper. Bring to a simmer and reduce the heat to low, placing a lid on top of the pan. Cook over low heat for about 10 minutes, stirring once, until the leeks have softened.

4 Sprinkle in the flour and carefully stir into the leeks. Then, add the cream, broth and horseradish and bring to the boil. Add more salt and pepper, if needed, then shut off the heat and pour the leek mix into the casserole dish.

5 Sprinkle panko crumbs over the top of the leeks and then the crumbled Stilton cheese. Dot the top with 1 tablespoon of butter. Lay the Pancetta pieces on the top and bake in the oven for about 15 minutes or until the leeks are golden brown and hot.

STICKY TOFFEE PUDDING WITH CLOTTED CREAM

A CLASSIC ENGLISH DESSERT AND A FAVORITE OF HER ROYAL HIGHNESS THE DUCHESS OF CAMBRIDGE. SERVES 6

FOR THE SAUCE
1 ½ packed cups dark brown sugar (Muscovado sugar is best)

1 cup unsalted butter

½ cup + 1 tablespoon heavy cream

FOR THE PUDDING
1 cup + 2 tablespoons chopped dates

1 teaspoon baking soda

½ pint boiling water

4 tablespoons butter

1 cup granulated sugar

1 teaspoon vanilla paste or extract

1 egg

2 cups + 2 tablespoons all purpose flour

1 teaspoon baking powder

1 quart capacity English pudding basin or casserole dish, greased

1 Prepare the sauce first by adding all of the ingredients to a heavy bottomed pan. Stir over high heat until everything is combined. Bring to a boil and simmer for 4 minutes. Pour about 1 ½ cups of the sauce into the greased pudding basin or casserole dish and allow to cool. Save the remaining sauce to pour over the finished pudding.

2 **FOR THE PUDDING** Place the dried dates in a bowl with the baking soda and the boiling water. Stir until the soda dissolves and leave to cool. This can be done a day ahead.

3 Cream the butter and sugar until light and fluffy, add the egg and vanilla and keep beating. Fold in the flour and baking powder followed by the date mix. Spoon the mix into the basin or casserole dish on top of the cold sauce.

4 **To steam the Pudding in a double boiler:** Place the pudding in a double boiler for about 1 ½ hours and until a skewer inserted into the pudding comes out clean. Don't forget to check the double boiler from time to time making sure there is water in the bottom. When the pudding is ready, reheat the remaining sauce. Invert the pudding onto a warm plate and pour over the sauce. Serve with clotted cream, whipped cream or ice cream.

5 **To bake the Pudding in the oven:** Preheat the oven to 350°F. Cover the top of the casserole dish with a sheet of parchment paper and then a layer of aluminum foil. Fold it loosely on the top of the casserole dish. Once covered, place the casserole in the middle shelf of the oven for about 30-40 minutes or until a skewer inserted in the middle comes out clean. Carefully remove the pudding from the oven, remove the parchment and aluminum foil and spoon the pudding onto warm serving plates. Pour the sauce over top and serve along with whipped or clotted cream, or ice cream.

A POT OF SOUP, A LOAF OF BREAD

Homemade soup makes you feel good all over, especially when it's slowly simmered and carefully tended. Add to that the fact that it is healthy and delicious and it's no wonder that people feel quite pampered when you set a large steaming bowl of soup in front of them. Best of all is that soup is so flexible that I use recipes more as guidelines than as hard and fast rules. I encourage you to do the same. If you see a recipe for black bean soup, think of it as "any bean" soup. Or a recipe for cream of asparagus soup can become "cream of any green" soup. Use what you have and what you love. That always works.

I've included three of our family favorites here along with a recipe for cheese biscuits to go along. If time is tight, you can always just pick up a baguette from your local bakery and a package of Irish butter. Best of all, these recipes make enough soup so that you are bound to have leftovers for a quick evening meal or weekday lunch.

CHIPOTLE, KALE & TURKEY MEATBALL SOUP

MAKES 4 PORTIONS

FOR THE SOUP

2 tablespoons olive oil

2 medium onions, peeled, halved and sliced

1 tablespoon minced garlic

4 cups (I bunch) fresh kale, stems removed and chopped into bite size pieces

2 (32 ounce) cartons of chicken broth

2 dried chipotle peppers (optional)

1 (14 ounce) can diced tomatoes (including juice)

1 (15 ounce) can great northern beans (drained and rinsed)

1 cup fresh (roughly) chopped cilantro

Salt

FOR THE MEATBALLS

1 pound ground turkey

1 tablespoon chipotle chili powder (to taste) or use regular chili powder

½ cup panko (or breadcrumbs)

1 egg

2 teaspoons salt

1 Add the olive oil, onions and garlic to a large pan with a pinch of salt and sauté until the onions are soft. Add the kale, broth, tomatoes and chipotle peppers and bring the soup to a boil. Reduce to a simmer while you prepare the meatballs.

2 Mix together the turkey, chili powder, salt, panko and egg until combined. Using a 1-inch ice cream scoop, or a tablespoon, drop the meatballs into the soup. Stir gently. (Use as few or many of the meatballs as you choose. Freeze any remaining meatballs).

3 Remove the 2 chipotle peppers from the soup and discard. Simmer the soup with meatballs for 10 to 15 minutes, until the meatballs are cooked through and then add the great northern beans and cilantro. Simmer a few minutes longer and taste and adjust seasonings.

4 Serve with warm crusty bread.

» *Chipotle, Kale & Turkey Meatball Soup, page 130*

CHEESE BISCUITS

THESE BISCUITS ARE EASY TO MAKE AND VERY EASY TO EAT. For the flakiest biscuits, make sure you don't overwork the dough. MAKES 8 BISCUITS

3 cups all purpose flour

1 ½ tablespoons baking powder

½ teaspoon soda

¼ teaspoon celery seeds

1 teaspoon salt

1 teaspoon sugar

¾ cup butter (6 ounces)

½ cup crumbled Stilton cheese

¼ cup chopped walnuts

1 cup buttermilk

1   Preheat the oven to 400°F.

2   In a large bowl add the flour, baking powder, soda, celery seeds, salt and sugar and stir together. Rub in the butter to make fine crumbs and then add the stilton and walnuts. Stir in the buttermilk to make a shaggy ball of dough.

3   Roll out to about 1-inch thick and cut into 2 ½-inch rounds using a biscuit cutter. Place on a baking sheet and bake in the center of the oven until brown, about 15 minutes. Remove from the oven and cool slightly before serving.

AVOCADO & PEA SOUP WITH LUMP CRAB

MAKES 4 PORTIONS

1 medium leek, white and light green parts only, washed well and chopped

1 medium onion, diced finely

2 tablespoons butter

1 tablespoon flour

1 pound frozen peas

3 cups chicken broth

½ avocado

4 ounces lump crabmeat

1 teaspoon lemon juice

¼ teaspoon finely minced ginger

¼ cup heavy cream, partly whipped

2 teaspoons fresh mint, chopped

2 slices Pancetta, torn into bite size pieces and deep fried until crisp

1 Finely chop the leek and onion and sauté in a large pan with the butter until soft. Stir in the flour and peas and add the chicken broth. Bring the soup to a boil and then simmer for about 15 minutes. Puree the soup and pass through a coarse sieve. Adjust the seasoning and set aside and keep warm until ready to serve.

2 Dice the avocado and set aside. In a small bowl add the crab, lemon juice and ginger and mix together. Place the crab in the center of four soup bowls in a pile and arrange the avocado around the bottom of the bowl. Bring the soup to a boil and pour into the bowl but not over the crab. Garnish the soup with a small dollop of cream, a sprinkle of mint and shards of the pancetta just before serving.

(ALMOST) FAT FREE VEGETABLE SOUP WITH TARRAGON CREAM

SERVES 4

1 yellow onion

3 large carrots

2 medium leeks (white and light green part),
washed well

1 rutabaga, peeled and diced

4 medium parsnips, peeled and diced

4 ribs celery

6 cups fat free chicken broth

1 teaspoon dried thyme

3 bay leaves

Salt and pepper to taste

2 tablespoons fresh tarragon, chopped

½ cup fat free Greek yogurt

1 Peel the onion, carrots, leeks, rutabaga and
   parsnips and chop into chunks about 1-2 inches.
   You should end up with about 2 cups of each
   vegetable. Cut the ends off the celery and chop
   the ribs into the same size pieces as the other
   vegetables. Place into a large, heavy based pan.

2 Pour the broth over the vegetables and add the
   thyme and bay leaves. Bring to a boil over high
   heat and reduce to a simmer for about 1 hour or
   until all of the vegetables are fork tender.

3 Remove the bay leaves and carefully puree the
   soup in a blender until smooth and creamy.
   Return to the pan and adjust the seasoning.
   Place over a low heat to keep the soup warm.

4 Fold the tarragon through the Greek yogurt
   and just before serving place a teaspoon of the
   tarragon cream on to the top of each bowl of
   soup. Serve with lots of whole wheat crusty bread.

AN ELEGANT TEA

No apologies here—this tea menu is quintessentially British. And that is how it should be! I've included some of the favorite tea cakes and sandwich fillings enjoyed by her Majesty. Since I have made each of these what seems like a million times, I can honestly say that each recipe is perfect. Potted shrimp is likely the most unfamiliar dish here for Americans but it really is a terrific addition to anyone's favorite tea recipe list. Basically it is a well-seasoned dish of chopped cooked shrimp is preserved under a thin layer of clarified butter. Spread thinly on toast, it is a rich buttery bite to be sure, and a little goes a long way.

Of course there is nothing fixed about a "traditional" English tea. It can be lavishly appointed tiered trays filled with delicate sandwiches, painstakingly decorated tarts and clouds of whipped cream, or just a simple plate of freshly cut shortbread. But you must have a nicely brewed pot of tea to go along. It's not that difficult even for novice tea makers to brew a great pot. Here are some simple pointers:

- Start with fresh cold water in a kettle
- Preheat your teapot by pouring some of the hot kettle water into the pot, swishing it around and discarding it. Now the pot's interior has been warmed up and the finished tea won't cool too quickly.
- Use high quality loose tea and just toss it into the bottom of your teapot. Not too much either. With standard black tea leaves, you want a thin layer of tea leaves across the bottom of your teapot. If you find the finished product too weak, just continue adding more tea leaves to subsequent pots until you find your perfect tea strength.
- Pour boiling water over the tea leaves, leave the lid off and wait. Two to three minutes is a good place to start and up to five minutes if you like a strong brew. When you are ready to drink, place the lid on the pot and pour the tea through a strainer into your (already warmed) cup or mug. Add milk and/or sugar to taste.

Now where are those shortbreads?

POTTED SHRIMP

2 sticks unsalted butter

¼ teaspoon nutmeg

⅛ teaspoon cayenne pepper

¼ teaspoon allspice

8 ounces peeled cooked shrimp (90/110 count—the tiny bay shrimp that you would use for shrimp salad)

1 stick salted butter

½ teaspoon lemon juice

Toast points, to serve alongside

1 Melt the unsalted butter in a sauté pan until hot and the foam has subsided. Mix in the nutmeg, cayenne and allspice. Pour over the shrimp and cook until shrimp and stir. Spoon into the ramekins. Refrigerate until the butter/shrimp mixture is firm.

2 Melt the remaining butter and stir in the lemon juice. Spoon this protective butter layer over the potted shrimp and refrigerate until set.

3 Serve with warm toast.

MACADAMIA BUTTERSCOTCH BARS

A TYPICAL TEA MENU COMBINES BOTH SAVORY AND SWEET DISHES AND WHILE I LIKE CHOCOLATE (A LOT) I'M NOT ALWAYS CONVINCED THAT IT GOES WELL WITH A NICE POT OF ENGLISH BREAKFAST TEA OR EARL GREY. By contrast, these macadamia bar cookies combining nuts, brown sugar and butterscotch complement a well brewed cup beautifully. MAKES 12 GOOD SIZE BAR COOKIES

1 ½ sticks unsalted butter

1 cup brown sugar

⅔ cup granulated sugar

2 eggs

1 ½ teaspoon maple syrup

1 ½ cups flour

1 teaspoon baking powder

1 pinch salt

1 cup chopped macadamia nuts

1 cup butterscotch chips

1 Preheat the oven to 350°F. Grease an 11x9 inch baking sheet.

2 Cream the butter and both sugars in a mixer until pale and fluffy. Add the eggs and maple syrup and beat until combined.

3 Fold in the flour, baking powder and salt followed by the nuts and butterscotch chips and spread into the prepared baking sheet.

4 Bake for about 30-40 minutes until golden brown. Allow to cool before slicing into bars.

LAVENDER SHORTBREAD

MAKES ABOUT 8-10 PORTIONS OF SHORTBREAD

1 ½ cups flour

¾ cup cornstarch

Zest of 1 lemon

2 teaspoons lavender flowers, fresh or dried

1 cup powdered sugar

2 sticks unsalted butter

¼ cup sugar

1 teaspoon lavender flowers fresh or dried

1 shortbread pan (If you don't have a shortbread pan you can roll out the dough ½-inch thick and use cookie cutters)

1 Preheat the oven to 350°F.

2 Sift the flour, cornstarch, lemon zest, lavender flowers and sugar into a large bowl. Cut the butter into small pieces and rub the butter and flour mixture between your fingers until it starts to form a shaggy ball of dough.

3 Lightly dust a shortbread pan with flour and press the paste into the pan. Trim off any excess and prick the top of the shortbread all over with a fork. This will help with cooking the shortbread evenly.

4 Bake for about 20 minutes until golden brown. Remove from the oven and cut the shortbread into wedges, but only going ⅓ of the way through. Sprinkle with granulated sugar and lavender flowers and place on a cooling wire to cool completely.

» *Lavender Shortbread, page 142*

COCKTAILS & CANAPÉS

I love cocktail and canapé parties. They are creative, inexpensive (if you don't splurge on the Osetra) and a relaxed way to mingle with all of your guests. The secret to canapé parties is planning and preparing ahead. Most nibbles can be put together before guests arrive, leaving you plenty of free time. At Buckingham Palace we had one event a year where we had to make 15,000 canapés, and if that doesn't teach you the importance of advance planning, then nothing will. It was an amazing feat of coordination. This menu is thankfully much simpler but full of flavor and variety. Don't forget to be creative with the drinks too. I always have beer and wine on hand, but I love putting together a tray of cocktails, just to mix things up a bit.

CRAB BEIGNETS

THIS RECIPE USES A PATE A CHOUX DOUGH THAT, WHEN DONE RIGHT, USES THE POWER OF STEAM TO PUFF UP, WHETHER IN THE OVEN, HOT OIL OR BOILING WATER. The dough has no special leavening agents; it's just made from water, milk, butter, flour, salt, sugar and eggs. The combination of crab, Old Bay and a touch of Gruyere also means you will never have leftovers, no matter the size of the party. MAKES 30 CANAPÉ SIZE

1 ¼ cups water

4 ounces butter (½ stick)

1 cup all purpose flour, sifted—(This is one of those recipes where sifting is fairly important. You want to avoid any clumps in your dough.)

4 eggs, room temperature

1 pound lump crab (fresh or canned)

4 ounces Gruyere cheese—grated

Salt and pepper to taste

Old Bay seasoning—to taste

2-3 cups neutral vegetable oil (for frying)

1 Put the water and butter in a pan and bring to a boil, melting the butter completely. Once it comes to a full simmer, quickly add the flour, remove the pan from the heat and stir with a wooden spoon until the flour is incorporated and the mixture leaves the sides of the pan, about a minute or two. You may notice a slight film forming at the bottom of the pan, a good indicator that the dough is dry. Remove the dough from the stove and set it aside to cool for a minute.

2 Begin adding the eggs. Transfer the dough to a mixer fitted with a standard paddle attachment (you can also do this by hand, transferring the dough to a larger bowl and using a wooden spoon). On low speed, begin stirring the dough and add the first egg. Immediately the dough will break up, become shiny and make slapping noises against the side of the bowl. Continue mixing and the dough will start to come together and lose that shiny look. When that happens, it is time to add the second egg. Proceed like this with each egg, until all four have been added. While the mixture is still warm, fold in the cheese, lumps of crab and season well with Old Bay, salt and pepper.

3 In a sauce pan or small wok, heat the oil to 350°F. Drop spoonfuls of the mixture measuring about a 1 ½ tablespoons each into the oil and cook until golden, about 3-4 minutes. Don't crowd the pan and fry the fritters in batches. Drain on paper towels and serve immediately.

SMOKED PORK & CILANTRO PANCAKES WITH JALAPEÑO CREAM CHEESE & PEACH JAM

MAKES ABOUT 30 APPETIZER PANCAKES

FOR THE PANCAKES

½ cup blue cornmeal (regular cornmeal is also fine)

½ cup all purpose flour

2 teaspoons baking powder

½ teaspoon salt

1 tablespoon sugar

1 egg

¾ cup milk

½ cup finely chopped cilantro

½ cup finely chopped green onions

Corn oil, for the griddle

1 cup whipped cream cheese

1 jalapeño, finely diced, with or without seeds depending upon your heat tolerance

8 ounces smoked pork or chicken—shredded (I buy 1 pound of smoked meat from my favorite BBQ restaurant and freeze in small bags until I need it)

½ cup peach jam

Cilantro to garnish

1 In a large bowl, mix all of the pancake ingredients together. Heat and lightly grease a skillet with the corn oil and spoon the pancake mix into the pan. Cook for about 1 minute until brown on the bottom and then turn over to cook on the other side for a further minute. Remove to a cooling rack.

2 Fold the diced jalapeño into the cream cheese and spoon onto the pancakes. Top with the shredded meat and finish with a little peach jam or chutney. Garnish with cilantro.

CROQUES MONSIEUR

AS A CHEF FOR OVER THIRTY YEARS I KNOW THAT YOU ONLY GET OUT OF THE OVEN WHAT YOU PUT INTO IT. Buying the best quality ingredients you can afford really does make a difference. Here, with the best ham and the best cheese you end up with the best grilled cheese. So very, very good... MAKES 16 PIECES (AS A CANAPÉ)

4 slices good quality ham (Panonia is my favorite. A little dry, slightly smoky and delicious but if you can't find that then a good quality Black Forest ham will work)

8 slices Gruyere cheese

½ stick of salted butter (softened, but not melted)

8 slices European style white bread

1 Preheat broiler to high if planning to serve straight away.

2 Butter the 8 slices of bread on one side. On four of them place a slice of Gruyere. Place a slice of ham on top of the cheese followed by another slice of Gruyere on top of the ham. Finish by laying the remaining bread (butter side down) on top of the cheese.

3 With the remaining butter, butter the outside of the bread on both sides and then place onto a baking sheet. If you plan to serve them straight away, place under the broiler for about 5 minutes until the bread turns golden brown and crispy.

4 Remove the tray from the broiler and brown the other side. Remove from the oven, discard the crusts and cut into 4 rectangle pieces. Serve immediately.

» *Croques Monsieur, page 148*

» *Kashmiri Chicken Curry, page 153*

A FAVORITE FAMILY CURRY

In the Anglo-Indian writer Salman Rushdie's novel "The Satanic Verses" one of the main characters, Gibreel, considers the benefits of turning London in to a steamy tropical Indian city. Such transformation would now include the scent of curry pots bubbling away in every neighborhood, along with the smell of toasting cumin, coriander and chilies wafting through the air from Whitechapel to Kensington. Reading that always makes my mouth water. I love a good curry of almost any provenance, be it Indian, Thai, Indonesian or even just a mongrelized English curry. So coming up with a favorite family curry was really just too difficult. Instead I've decided to narrow the choices down to my top three. I think they are all perfectly delicious, though I'm mindful that curry is a very personal thing. Fiddle around with the spicing until you find the flavor that suits you best.

AN ENGLISH LAMB CURRY

WHEN QUEEN VICTORIA WAS ON THE THRONE AND BRITAIN STILL HAD AN EMPIRE THERE WERE TWO INDIAN CHEFS EMPLOYED IN THE ROYAL KITCHENS WHOSE SOLE JOB WAS TO MAKE A CURRY EVERY DAY FOR THE ROYAL TABLE. "Curry powder" as we know it was created for the western market—a blend of spices that includes coriander, turmeric, cumin, fenugreek, ginger, garlic, fennel seed, cardamom, nutmeg, red pepper and cinnamon. This is a super easy stew to put together and is only mildly spicy. The addition of tomato paste and bouillon cubes makes it authentically English! MAKES 4 PORTIONS

2 pounds leg of lamb cut into 1-inch cubes

2 tablespoons olive oil

1 large onion, chopped

2 cloves garlic, crushed

¼ cup curry powder

¼ cup flour

1 tablespoon tomato paste

3 cups water

3 beef bouillon cubes (knorr)

1 apple, peeled and chopped

1 tablespoon mango chutney

Kosher salt and ground black pepper

1 Heat the oil in a heavy based pan over a high heat and add the beef. Stir until the meat all turns brown and remove to a colander with a slotted spoon to strain off excess fat. Add the onions and garlic to the fat in the pan and cook until the onions start to soften. Stir in the curry powder and let that powder toast a bit with the onions and garlic, but don't let it burn.

2 Return the meat to the pan and stir in the flour and tomato paste. Give it all a good stir. Gradually add the water and broth cubes and keep stirring to avoid any lumps of flour. When you have a nice smooth sauce, add the chopped apple, place a lid on the pan, turn the flame down low and let the stew simmer for approximately 1 hour or until the meat is fork tender.

3 Add the mango chutney to taste. It should provide a tangy, sweet, spicy shot of flavor to the stew. Season well with the salt and pepper. Serve with basmati rice and papadums.

KASHMIRI CHICKEN CURRY

INDIAN FOOD IS MY FAVORITE CUISINE TO BOTH EAT AND COOK. People say it's spicy, but it's not. Rather it is a palette of ingredients joined together to create an amazing dish and, like an orchestra, each ingredient has its part to play. These days the British passion for "a good curry" has never been stronger and there are occasional government warnings of a growing shortage of Indian chefs to cook all those lovely dishes. No worry for the home cooks though, we can easily make our own!

I use chicken thighs for this recipe but you can use chicken breast. Just cut it into cubes. The spices are fairly specific so you can either buy them online or jot over to your nearest Indian grocer and stock up. The Kashmiri chili powder is quite hot, so make adjustments as you see fit.

I like to make this dish over two days and eat it over a week. The spices absorb into the meat overnight and it tastes better the next day... and the next. MAKES 4 PORTIONS

FOR THE MARINADE AND SAUCE
6 cardamoms, brown or black, seeds only

2 cloves

2 cloves garlic, minced

1 large onion, diced

2 tomatoes, diced

2 tablespoons fresh chopped ginger

1 tablespoon Kashmiri chili powder (or to taste)

2 teaspoons Garam Masala

½ teaspoon turmeric powder

1 teaspoon ground cumin

1 teaspoon salt

FOR THE CURRY
12 chicken thighs (boneless, skinless)

¼ cup vegetable oil or Ghee

2 cinnamon sticks

½ cup water

¼ cup cashews, ground

½ cup plain yogurt

¼ cup chopped cilantro

Salt and pepper to taste

1 Place all the marinade ingredients together and mix. Place them in a large ziplock bag and add the chicken thighs. Refrigerate overnight.

2 Heat the oil or ghee in a large sauté pan over high heat and add the chicken, marinade, water and cinnamon sticks. Simmer gently until the chicken is tender, about 20 minutes. Adjust the seasoning with salt. Stir in the ground cashews and yogurt and simmer. At this point, do not let the stew boil. You just want to warm the yogurt. Garnish with the cilantro and serve over hot rice.

THAI SHRIMP CURRY

SOME CURRIES REALLY BENEFIT FROM A LONG SLOW COOK WITH THE MEAT ABSORBING THE FLAVOR OF THE SAUCE. Not this one though. Using shrimp, this curry is quick, easy to make, full of bright flavors and perfect served over rice or noodles. MAKES 4 PORTIONS

1 tablespoon sesame oil

1 cup onion, thinly sliced

1 red bell pepper, cut into bite size pieces

1 teaspoon garlic, minced

1 tablespoon chopped fresh ginger

2 pounds (21/25 count) peeled and deveined shrimp

¼ cup red Thai curry paste, Mae Ploy is a good brand

2 large tomatoes, diced

1 tablespoon brown sugar

1 teaspoon Thai fish sauce, or to taste

2 tablespoons crunchy peanut butter

1 teaspoon (or to taste) garlic chili sauce

½ cup chicken broth

1 (14 ounce) can unsweetened coconut milk

2 teaspoons lime juice

½ cup fresh chopped cilantro

½ cup green onions, finely chopped

1 Heat the sesame oil in a 12-inch skillet over medium heat and add the onions, pepper, garlic and ginger. Cook until the vegetables start to soften. Add the shrimp and stir. Cook for about 4 minutes until the shrimp are opaque. Stir in the curry paste, tomatoes, brown sugar, fish sauce, peanut butter and garlic chili sauce. Add the chicken broth and coconut milk and simmer. Adjust the seasoning with salt and pepper. Stir in the lime juice.

2 Pour over rice or noodles and garnish with the cilantro and green onions.

"FOOLPROOF" BASMATI RICE

I CALL THIS MY FOOLPROOF RICE RECIPE BECAUSE IT WORKS EVERY TIME AND MAKES THE FLUFFIEST RICE EVER. Don't be tempted to lift the lid before the 18 minutes is up.

MAKES 4 PORTIONS

1 tablespoon olive oil

1 cup basmati rice

2 cups chicken broth

½ onion, finely diced

½ cup sliced almonds

1 tablespoon butter

2 tablespoons cilantro, chopped

1 In a small saucepan bring the chicken broth to a boil. In a separate heavy based pan heat the olive oil and add the onion, sauté until it starts to soften and then stir in the rice. Add the chicken broth and stir. Bring the rice to a boil and reduce to a simmer. Place a lid on top and cook for 18 minutes or until all of the liquid has evaporated.

2 Remove the rice from the pan into a large bowl and fluff up the grains with a fork and adjust the seasoning.

3 In a frying pan melt the butter and add the almonds, cook until golden brown and pour over the rice. Garnish with the chopped cilantro.

» *Roasted Turkey with Pan Juices, page 159*

THANKSGIVING FOR A CROWD

Nineteen years ago when I moved to the America I had heard of Thanksgiving but never really knew what it was or why it was celebrated. The first couple of years I enjoyed the holiday by spending the extra day off relaxing with my wife and baby daughter. Once Kelly started pre-K and came home with drawings of her hand decorated to resemble a turkey and began asking, "Why don't we have turkey today like all of my friends?" I knew it was time to assimilate.

My employer, a wealthy Dallas family where I worked as a private chef, had been initially reluctant to foist Thanksgiving cooking duty on me, but there came one October day when I was told, "We want you to cater Thanksgiving for the family this year." I was given a list of dishes (about fifteen in all) the majority for which I was responsible. Family members were bringing some of the dishes because, "They always do." This was going to be a Texas Thanksgiving and frankly the list was incomprehensible to me. Why did people want to eat turkey in November when it was rightly served for Christmas lunch? Where was the delicious chestnut stuffing? Cornbread "dressing" instead? So it's not a stuffing? Cranberry jelly... Jelly? That must be a typo... I'm sure they meant fresh cranberries slowly simmered with grated orange zest and a little Cointreau to finish. Nope. Just open a can of cranberry jelly, slice and fan it onto a plate of butter lettuce. Next up—green bean casserole. Here were green beans cooked to within one inch of their life, strained and stirred into canned mushroom soup and then wait for it... topped with ready made onion rings. It took me fifteen minutes at a busy store the day before Thanksgiving trying to find ready-made onion rings. Where do they store them? Hint: Not with the fresh onions! Also on the list was asparagus, canned asparagus. I had never in thirty years of cooking ever bought a can of asparagus. I opened one end of the can and tipped the asparagus into my hand over the sink to allow the juices to run out. As I did, the heads of the asparagus fell off into the sink leaving me holding a can of mush and having to go back to the store for more.

Then there was a salad to go with the turkey, not so surprising except when I checked out the ingredient list. This was a black bing cherry salad with Coca-Cola and canned cherries and canned mandarins and everything else in the pantry that still had a good sell by date! Don't get me started on the mashed sweet potatoes with melted marshmallows on top. I couldn't wait to get home to a sensible lamb stew and mashed potatoes. While I really try to be quite ecumenical about food, preferring for us all just to get along, that Thanksgiving set me back several years in attempting my own household celebration.

Now, nineteen years later, I am a master at Thanksgiving lunch and if you promise not to tell anyone, I have to admit, once Kelly arrives home from college and the family is all together, it is truly one of my favorite meals of the year. Below are a few of my family's favorite Thanksgiving dishes. I hope they become your family's favorites too.

ROASTED TURKEY WITH PAN JUICES

MAKES 6 PORTIONS

1 Kosher turkey (10 to 12 pounds)

Coarse kosher salt

½ cup olive oil

1 tablespoon black pepper

2 onions, peeled and sliced

1 head of celery, rough chopped

12 garlic cloves

1 bunch fresh thyme

4 bay leaves

2 cups chicken or turkey broth

½ bottle dry white wine

1 stick unsalted butter

⅓ cup all purpose flour

1 Remove the turkey from the refrigerator an hour before you plan to cook. Preheat the oven to 450°F. Remove any giblets from the cavity and reserve for the gravy. Pat the turkey dry with paper towel. Pour the olive oil over the turkey and massage so that all of the bird is covered in oil. Sprinkle lightly with kosher salt and black pepper.

2 In the bottom of a large roasting pan, add the onion, giblets, turkey neck, celery, garlic, thyme and bay leaf. Place the turkey, breast side up the roasting pan on top of the vegetables. Pour the broth and wine over the vegetables.

3 Transfer pan to the oven and roast for 30 minutes. Reduce the oven temperature to 350°F and continue roasting until an instant-read thermometer inserted in the thickest part of a thigh reaches 165°F (about 2 ¼ hours)

4 Remove the turkey to a warm platter to rest for at least 30-45 minutes. In a large pan melt the butter and stir in the flour. Remove the vegetables, giblets and neck from the roasting pan and add the liquid to the butter and flour to make the gravy. Season with salt and pepper.

» *Shredded Brussel Sprouts with Onions & Bacon, page 160*

OLD ENGLISH APPLE PIE

WHO DOESN'T LOVE APPLE PIE? I GREW UP EATING ALL SORTS OF APPLE PIES, TARTS AND TURNOVERS AND AS A YOUNG CHEF GOT A CHANCE TO FORAGE THROUGH SOME OF THE MOST GLORIOUS ORCHARDS IN ENGLAND—THOSE BELONGING TO THE QUEEN. How I yearn for the delicious Bramley apples exclusive to where I grew up in Nottinghamshire in the UK, some the size of two fists together, sweet and fluffy when cooked. They made the best apple pies in the world.

In this recipe I've listed Granny Smiths which are readily available and make a tasty pie filling. But don't feel too bound by that. Your local farmer's market might have some great varieties to try and since apples lend themselves well to mixing and matching you can certainly add more than one kind of apple to your pie. For the pastry dough, creaming the butter and sugar together in this recipe along with the high proportion of fat to flour and the addition of egg makes this a rich and crunchy pastry rather than the traditional flaky pastry. MAKES 6 PORTIONS

FOR THE PASTRY
2 ½ sticks butter

¾ cup sugar

1 egg

1 teaspoon vanilla paste or extract

3 cups flour

FOR THE FILLING
4 granny smiths apples

½ cup granulated sugar

¼ cup Muscovado (or light brown) sugar

⅓ cup raisins

½ stick butter, melted and cooled

1 lemon, juice and zest

1 orange, juice and zest

½ teaspoon ground nutmeg

1 teaspoon cinnamon

1 egg, beaten

1 Preheat an oven to 350°F.

2 In a mixing bowl cream the butter and sugar until smooth and add the egg and vanilla paste. Add the flour and blend until combined. Refrigerate for at least 1 hour before use.

3 Peel, quarter and remove the core from the apples and slice. Place the apples in a large bowl and add the granulated sugar, muscovado sugar, raisins, melted butter, lemon and orange zest and juice, nutmeg and cinnamon. Stir until combined.

4 Roll out the pastry and line a 9 inch by 1 ½ flan ring. Place the apple filling inside and using a pastry brush, brush the edge of the pastry with the beaten egg. Roll out a circle of pastry to cover the pie and trim the edges. Brush the remaining egg over the top of the pie.

5 Bake in the center of the oven for about 40 minutes or until the pastry is golden brown.

TECHNIQUE
SPOTLIGHT

Turkey Brining & Roasting

I have teenagers in my house these days, so to take a page from their questionable musical choices and because I fancy myself quite hip, I give my turkey the moniker "the notorious GBD"—cue the eye roll from my son. GBD is short for "golden, brown and delicious" and that is exactly what you want from a turkey on Thanksgiving. Now while I've had turkey prepared all sorts of ways—smoked (very nice), deep fried (terrifying), and grilled (a bit fiddly)—I do think a roasted turkey is best. Done right, you get juicy succulent meat, incredible kitchen smells and a lovely photo op before everyone sits down. Here are some tips I use when roasting up a bird.

• I'm partial to a Kosher bird which comes presalted, is always juicy and tender and doesn't require any further brining. However I know there are lots and lots of turkey choices out there and if you can't find a Kosher bird, find one that is listed as "natural" turkey with 4-5% juices. Butterball usually sells a natural bird and isn't hard to find. Words like "organic," "free range" and "heirloom" are all good, but the level of juiciness may vary, so check with your butcher and see what he recommends.

• Dry Brining. If you do decide to give you turkey a little flavor boost, dry brining is simple and yields great results. For a 15 pound turkey make a quick herb salt of 3 tablespoons of salt, 1 tablespoon of dried crushed sage, 1 teaspoon of crushed thyme and 2 teaspoons of crushed rosemary. Place your turkey in a large plastic bag and sprinkle the herb salt all over, include a good bit inside the cavity. Close up the bag and place the turkey in the fridge, breast side down. Let it stay that way for 12-18 hours and flip the bird, breast side up for another 12-18 hours. Then remove the turkey from the plastic and set it on a rack in the fridge, uncovered, overnight. The skin will tighten up a bit and take on a beautiful bronze color as it roasts.

- To Truss or not to Truss. I'm in the "not truss" camp for the simple reason that air flow around the legs helps ensures even cooking. You don't want an overcooked breast and an undercooked leg/thigh.
- Go High then Low. Roast your turkey at 425-450°F for the first half hour and then down to 350-325°F for the remainder. I prefer to roast a turkey on a rack set over a roasting pan that has a few roughly chopped carrots, celery, onions and some of the turkey giblets in. Also, pour a bit of water or broth (two cups or so) on the bottom for the several hours of roasting. After that the bird itself will start yielding delicious basting juices.
- Baste and the baste some more. Every half an hour. No excuses!

And that is it. That lovingly basted turkey is ready when the thermometer reads 165°F in the thickest part of the thigh. Remove the turkey from the oven and let it sit for at least a half an hour before carving.

WINTER

Christmas is always a mad sprint for me. My catering company, Eating Royally Fine Dining, runs at a fevered pitch from holiday party to holiday party. My waitstaff are stretched to the limit and I'll have to call in extra hands. The prep chefs take bets on the size and number of events we will do, yet the actual number is always higher than even they imagine. The logistics of it all take over my life. Finally December 25th arrives and with it, a brief respite. Christmas is here and we are healthy and whole and together and I can't ask for more. I savor the day with my family, knowing that the upcoming week will be the final sprint of the year.

By New Year's Eve, my internal batteries are running low. Unless I'm catering an event, it is indeed rare for me to still be awake and watch the ball drop and fireworks light up the sky. I generally disappear off to bed and I can tell you I don't need much rocking to sleep. My last blissful thought before drifting off is that I have utterly nothing planned for tomorrow. I can sleep in late, pad about in my pajamas until lunch, FaceTime the family across the pond to wish them Happy New Year and watch sports during the afternoon. Like my fellow chef and cooks all over the world, I too utter the "chef's prayer" wherein we give our thanks and gratitude that the holidays are over. Praise the Lord.

Come January, I'll spend a week or two catching up backlogged letters and emails. Now there will be time for recipe testing and incorporating new ingredients into the spring menu. I can even get home in time to eat dinner with my family; a real luxury. Of course, I am the one that cooks dinner!

For so many reasons, winter is my favorite season. The weather is perfect and I try to enjoy every day of it, knowing that too soon the Texas heat will descend and I'll be wistful for crisp clear mornings. The sunsets are spectacular now, glowing hot pink and turquoise and stretching out forever. Best of all, the climate is mild enough for all-seasons gardening. I'm chuffed to be outside in January harvesting bunches of kale, spinach, carrots, parsley and dill. I make a point of calling my sister back in Nottinghamshire, teasing her about 'how the sunshine is a bit intense this morning" and she quickly responds "Oh, sod off." She's always had a way with words. It's not easy being in England during the winter, living under leaden grey skies for months on end with only the occasional seed catalogue to keep you going. But in the milder southern States there is an embarrassment of riches each season of the year and I'll admit to an enduring childlike wonder every time I plant a seed that, in short order, becomes healthy food for my family. Plus, that lovely winter garden soon translates into a kitchen filled with wonderful smells of some of my favorite foods—stews, curries and braises.

Deep down, I've always been a boy who loves a good stew. Slow braised meat in a rich sauce served over a plate of creamy mashed potatoes or soft polenta. It just doesn't get any better. I suspect it is the smell of stew that is almost as important to me as the taste. As a child I was fed often by a mother and grandmother who were by nature and necessity frugal cooks. Winter stews meant loads of vegetables like cabbage, potatoes, rutabagas (or swedes as we called them) and carrots, combined with just a small piece of cheap meat, braised slowly to break down the fatty collagen and kept under a tight lid to hold the juices and flavors in. Winter in the town of Newark where I grew up meant dark skies by 4 PM and on the weekends after playing soccer with my friends until we could no longer see the ball, I would trudge home and walk up to our tiny back porch, my breath a visible puff of steam in the cold air and my hands freezing. Opening that kitchen door, the light and smell would hit me straight on. It was a blast of warm air filling my nose with the gamy, earthy scent of lamb and veggie stew bubbling away on the stove. My mother would be there with a glass of cider in her hand saying, "Take your boots off, wash your hands and set the table. It's all nearly ready." What lovely words.

CHRISTMAS CELEBRATION FOR FAMILY & FRIENDS

I t was 75°F this past Christmas in Dallas. Again. As many years as I've lived here, I still can't get used to it. The sun is shining and the kids are in t shirts and flip flops. Extended family is far away and we automatically calculate the time difference to make sure we call everyone after Christmas lunch, sending our love and best wishes to each other with a heartfelt longing that always leaves a lump in my throat.

It's all so different from the cold Christmas mornings of my childhood. My memories of them are thick, fat ones. Waking up in the early morning darkness, always before my brother and sister and hearing the slow rhythmic snoring of my father. Padding about the house in my footed winter fleece (or worse yet, itchy winter woolens) to look downstairs at the tree and the presents underneath. Waiting, always waiting, for everyone to wake up and the day to get started. It seemed like forever before the sky outside the front bay window moved from inky black to a soft grey light and I could see bedroom lights go on in my friend's house across the street. I didn't dare touch the gifts piled about. Gift opening would happen later in the day and I'd be considered a spoiler by peeking.

Christmas is magical in England. Looking back I realize how lucky I was coming from a family whose parents and grandparents believed deeply in the importance of a child's Christmas. Granted, memory can be selective but my recollections of Christmas are suffused by an overwhelming sense of kindness. I come from kind people and as the years go by and I grow older, I remain deeply appreciative.

I can smell, see and hear it all so clearly. The rugged scent of roasted coffee and properly thick bacon sizzling in the frypan. A fruit salad of oranges and grapefruit cut clear of the pith, like shiny jewels in a bowl. Fruitcakes doused with whiskey (or rum) eaten thin slice after thin slice, until they seem to disappear. Pots of tea with crumbly scones. A roasting turkey in the oven so big my dad would joke every year "we are going to have to take the door off to get this one in." My Nan, mother and auntie busying away in the tiny kitchen mashing potatoes, parsnips and straining brussels sprouts, my Nan's eyeglasses steaming up. My grandmother's sideboard, groaning with puddings and a wobbling jelly (always a rabbit jelly mold—I think it was just the only jelly mold she had) and at the center, a ridiculously ornate trifle topped with a whipped cream mountain. Oh that trifle! We always made sure to save room.

I was always more interested in what was going on in the kitchen than playing party games with my brother and sister even at a young age. Of course when I got to Buckingham Palace and saw how the chefs there created a sumptuous holiday table, the McGrady celebration seemed rather homespun by comparison... but I'll defend it to the end. It was wonderful to be a McGrady child at Christmas.

These days our Christmas meal is a study of American-European goodwill. There is beef bourguignon with its roots in French cookery and its timeless comforting appeal to stew loving Americans. The accompanying potato pie references the English love of savory tarts, rich with cream and potatoes but with the addition of amazing California crafted Humboldt Fog cheese.

At the end of the day, our family is English and for dessert we must have a trifle. Sometimes I make a traditional one with layers of sherry soaked vanilla sponge, jello, blancmange and custard. Other years, our trifle is both fancy and fanciful with layers of chocolate sponge cake drizzled with Baileys, whipped cream, pears and a crumbled heath bar replacing the chocolate flake bar of my mother's. And yes, a lovely dollop of whipped cream on top to make everyone smile.

Merry Christmas to you all.

» *Beef Bourguignon, page 173*

BEEF BOURGUIGNON

THIS DISH IS A FRENCH CLASSIC THAT IS BECOMING MORE AND MORE POPULAR HERE AT CHRISTMAS. Whenever I make this dish I always double the recipe, planning to freeze half for later. Well, that rarely happens with guests coming back for seconds and even thirds. It is that delicious. Please buy the best beef chuck your wallet can afford and look for deep marbling throughout the muscle. It is that marbling that makes the final stew so succulent and satisfying.

It is traditionally served over noodles but I just love serving this alongside a steaming hot bowl of mashed potatoes or a wedge of rich potato pie. The recipe below serves four, but can be scaled up easily for a larger crowd. MAKES 4 PORTIONS

2 pounds beef chuck, diced into large chunks about 2 inches wide

¼ cup vegetable oil

Salt and pepper

⅓ cup flour

1 cup smoked thick cut bacon cut into ¼ inch strips, about ⅓ to ½ of a pound

1 ½ cups red wine (I prefer Zinfandel, but any nice red will do)

1 ½ cups beef broth

2 cups mushrooms—quartered

1 cup of peeled pearl onions

½ cup chopped parsley

1 In a large skillet heat the oil until smoking hot. Dry the beef off with a paper towel and season generously with salt and pepper. Carefully add the beef to the pan and sauté until brown on all sides. Don't crowd the pan, leaving room between the pieces so they can properly brown and not steam. Brown in batches, if necessary. Strain the beef into a colander, discarding the oil.

2 Place the beef into a large eight-quart heavy pot and stir in the flour. Add the bacon, red wine and broth and stir. You want the meat to be almost fully submerged in liquid. Add the quartered mushrooms and pearl onions and bring the pot briefly to a boil on the stovetop. Stir once more, reduce the heat to gentle simmer and place a lid on the pan. Stir the meat every fifteen minutes. Alternatively, you can place the covered pot in a low 325°F oven, again checking every 15 minutes and giving it a good stir to prevent any sticking or burning. Cook until the beef is fork tender, about 2 hours. Pour into a serving dish and garnish with chopped parsley.

HUMBOLDT FOG & GREEN ONION POTATO PIE

THE PIE CRUST CAN BE MADE UP TO TWO DAYS IN ADVANCE AND PLACED TIGHTLY WRAPPED IN PLASTIC IN YOUR REFRIGERATOR. Let it warm up slightly on the kitchen counter before you start rolling it out. This dough is enough to make a large 9 inch tart with a bottom and top crust.

MAKES 6 PORTIONS

FOR THE PIE CRUST
4 ½ cups all-purpose flour

1 stick (4 ounce) unsalted butter

½ cup shortening, vegetable or lard

½ teaspoon salt

½ cup ice cold water

3 pounds yukon gold potatoes, peeled and sliced thin

1 tablespoon olive oil

½ yellow onion, thinly sliced

1 clove garlic, minced

2 eggs

1 egg yolk

1 cup heavy cream

⅓ cup green onion, finely chopped

1 cup sharp cheddar, grated (about 5 ounces)

1 cup Humboldt fog, crumbled (about 5 ounces)

Salt and pepper

1 egg, beaten, for brushing the pastry

One 9 inch loose bottomed fluted tart tin

1 **TO MAKE THE DOUGH** In a large bowl, add the flour and rub in the butter and shortening to make fine crumbs. Alternatively, you can make the dough in your food processor, pulsing a few times to incorporate the flour with the butter/ shortening. Then dump out the butter/flour mixture into a large bowl. Stir in the water and gather up the dough to form a ball. If the dough still looks too dry and won't come together into a ball, add more water, one tablespoon at a time. Divide the dough into two balls, one twice as large as the other (a ⅔ ball and a ⅓ ball). Wrap each ball in plastic wrap and refrigerate for an hour (or up to two days).

2 **FOR THE FILLING** Cover the thinly sliced potatoes with cold water in a large pan and bring to the boil. Simmer for 5 minutes and strain. Allow the potatoes to cool.

3 In a medium skillet saute the onion and garlic in the olive oil until they start to soften. Set aside to cool briefly. In a separate large bowl, combine the beaten eggs, yolk, cream, green onion. Add in the sautéed onion and garlic. Whisk until combined and stir in both cheeses. Set aside.

» Caramel Chocolate Trifle, page 176

RING IN THE NEW YEAR

New Year's Eve dinner is about spending time with your guests and relaxing. After all, it is your party too! So these recipes are designed to be prepared ahead of time so that when your guests arrive for dinner you are just "popping things in the oven"

You can bake the first part of your soufflés the day ahead or in the morning and turn them out on to a tray so they are oven ready. The cherry fennel jam can be made a week ahead too. The salmon can be sitting in the fridge on a baking sheet with the sriracha mayonnaise and chia seeds already on it. I often roast some fingerling potatoes to go along with the salmon and I make sure to roast them earlier in the day, so that all you have to do is slide them into the oven when you put the salmon in to cook.

In Scotland, New Years Eve is called Hogmanay and I've chosen a Scottish Cranachan for dessert. You can prepare it ahead of time in martinis glasses or even ramekins. Of course The Queen always spends New Year's Eve at Sandringham so this recipe of Sandringham Oranges is perfect to garnish the Cranachan. It too can be made several days ahead.

I like to serve dessert at midnight with a splash of whisky over the oranges and Cranachan. Happy New Year!

TWICE BAKED GOAT CHEESE SOUFFLÉS

MAKES 6 SOUFFLÉS

½ stick softened unsalted butter for greasing the ramekins

½ cup grated parmesan cheese for lining the ramekins

3 ½ tablespoons unsalted butter

⅓ cup all purpose flour

1 ⅓ cups milk

4 eggs (separated)

Pinch of grated nutmeg

2 teaspoons Dijon mustard

1 teaspoon finely chopped fresh thyme leaves

Salt and pepper to taste

8 ounces goat cheese, crumbled

¾ cup heavy cream (for the twice baking)

1 teaspoon finely chopped fresh thyme leaves

2 cups baby arugula

CHERRY FENNEL JAM

1 fennel bulb, finely chopped

1 small onion finely diced

1 cup fresh cherries, pitted and chopped

⅔ cup light brown sugar

½ cup apple vinegar

½ teaspoon fennel seeds

salt and pepper to taste

1 Preheat the oven to 375°F and butter six ¾ cup ramekins. Line the ramekins with the grated cheese.

2 In a saucepan, melt the butter and whisk in the flour. Gradually add the milk and then bring the mix to a boil. Remove the pan from the heat and add the egg yolks, nutmeg, mustard, 1 teaspoon of thyme, salt and pepper and ⅔ of the cheese and whisk until the cheese is melted.

3 Beat the egg whites until stiff and fold into the soufflé mix with the remaining goat cheese. Divide the mixture between the ramekins and arrange on a large baking sheet so that the edges of the ramekins are not touching. Add hot water to the baking sheet to reach halfway up the sides of the ramekins and bake in the middle of the oven until slightly puffed and golden brown, about 15 minutes.

4 Cherry Fennel Jam In a large pan add all of the jam ingredients and simmer with a lid on for about 40 minutes stirring occasionally. Cook until the liquid has reduced and the fennel, onion and cherries are soft. Set aside to cool.

5 At this stage the soufflés may either be served straight away or used later and "twice baked" If the latter, then continue with directions below.

6 Remove from the oven and let the soufflés sink back into the ramekins for about 30 minutes.

7 Increase the oven temperature to 425°F. Lightly butter a baking sheet, carefully un-mold the soufflés and invert onto the baking sheet. Bake the soufflés until slightly puffed and heated through—about 5 minutes. While the soufflés are baking, bring the cream with the remaining thyme to a boil in a small pan and reduce slightly.

8 Transfer the soufflés to plates and spoon 2 tablespoons of cream over each. Sprinkle arugula leaves over the top and drizzle with the cherry fennel jam.

» *Twice Baked Goat Cheese Soufflés, page 180*

CHIA & SRIRACHA CRUSTED SALMON

I CAN'T TELL YOU HOW OFTEN I COOK SALMON. It's super healthy and reasonably priced. When you purchase it always ask for "center cut fillets" and then ask if they would "remove a little of the belly." You won't always get the latter, but when you do, it's a nice saving and at least you will get four uniform pieces of fish that will now all cook at the same time. Chia seeds are found in most supermarkets and have been touted as a "superfood" i.e. rich in antioxidants and nutrients. I like them because they add a nutty flavor to this dish. If they aren't in your local shop, please feel free to use sesame seeds instead. MAKES 4 PORTIONS

4 eight ounce salmon fillets

¼ cup Sriracha mayonnaise (2 tablespoons Sriracha with 2 tablespoons mayonnaise)

½ cup Chia seeds

1 tablespoon olive oil

Salt and pepper

1 Preheat the oven to 400°F. Season the salmon fillets with salt and pepper and place on a baking sheet skin side down. Rub the olive oil on to the flesh of the salmon.

2 Divide the Sriracha mayo between the four salmon fillets and spread over the flesh (but not the skin). Sprinkle liberally the Chia seeds over the Sriracha sauce. At this point the fillets can be refrigerated on their baking sheet, ready to go in the oven.

3 When ready to bake, allow fillets to come to room temperature on your counter, about 30 minutes. Slide them into the hot oven and bake on a center rack for about 12 minutes.

4 Remove from the oven and carefully lift the salmon off the baking sheet leaving the skin stuck to the sheet pan.

CRANACHAN

CRANACHAN, PRONOUNCED "KRANAKAN," IS A TYPICAL SCOTTISH DESSERT, BUT IT'S CONSIDERED UNUSUAL IN THE STATES. Maybe that is because we don't associate oatmeal with dessert, unless it is in the form of a cookie. This is actually a delicious, not too heavy, slightly boozy dessert that is a perfect way to ring in the New Year. Best of all, it's made earlier in the day and refrigerated. All ready for your celebration later. MAKES ABOUT 4 PORTIONS

½ cup coarse oatmeal, (steel cut or pin head) divided

1 cup + 2 tablespoons heavy cream

2-4 tablespoons Drambuie

Honey to taste

1 Toast the oatmeal in a sauté pan on a high heat until lightly brown. Then set aside to cool. Place ¼ cup of the oatmeal into a small bowl and stir in the Drambuie and about 1-2 tablespoons honey. Leave for about 15 minutes to soften the oats.

2 Whip the cream into a soft consistency and fold in the dry oatmeal. Next, fold in the soft drambuie soaked oatmeal, and test for sweetness. Add more honey if needed. Serve in tall glasses alternating with fresh berries or serve in a large bowl on it's own alongside a bowl of berries for your guests to build their own.

» *Cranachan, page 183,*
and Sandringham Oranges, page 185

SANDRINGHAM ORANGES

2 cups granulated sugar

2 cups water

3 large oranges

¼ cup Cointreau

1   Preheat the oven to 300°F. Bring the sugar and water to a rolling boil and boil for at least 5 minutes to make a syrup. Make sure all the sugar has melted and you have a clear, slightly thick liquid. Slice the oranges thin (about ¼ inch thick) with the skin on and fan into a casserole dish. Pour the syrup over the oranges so they are covered. And then cover the dish with aluminum foil or casserole lid. Bake in the oven for about 1 hour or until the skin of the oranges is tender. To test that the skin is soft, just poke it slightly with a skewer or fork. The skewer should pierce the rind easily with no resistance

2   Cool the orange slices in the syrup. When the dish is at room temperature, carefully remove the oranges to a plate and strain the syrup into a small saucepan. Over medium high heat, reduce the liquid in the saucepan to a glaze and add the Cointreau. Spoon the warm glaze over the oranges and let cool. Serve a slice or two on top of the Cranachan and if you are feeling convivial, top the whole dessert with a splash of whiskey.

SPOTLIGHT

The Garden: A Cook's Paradise

Curries, stews, braises, soups—all the wonderful winter dishes I love rely heavily on humble tubers, roots and greens that grow in the garden. I can't imagine cooking without them.

But growing up, I was never interested in plants. My mother was a keen gardener and on Sundays (her day off) she would spend most of it either in our garden or dragging me, my brother and my sister off to the local nursery for hours on end. I'd be bored silly and amuse myself bombarding the goldfish in the pond with gravel just so I could see how fast they swam.

Fast forward thirty years and to her amazement (and mine too) I am constantly calling her for tips on growing vegetables. I expect it was working for the Royal Family that taught me just how much the garden teaches and inspires creativity in a chef. At Balmoral, the gardener would deliver to the kitchen masses of carrots, cabbages, chard and sturdy bunches of leeks, dirt still clinging to their roots with delicate pearls of water weeping out of the newly cut dark green tops. Beets of all kinds, with their abundant leafy tops looked like something out of a still life painting. Those tops, shredded and sautéed with a little olive oil and garlic, salt and pepper and a dash of apple cider vinegar, made the most delicious, healthy side dish. The Balmoral raspberries were amazing too; plump fruit picked carefully off the canes in the afternoon just in time to serve with whipped cream inside crisp sweet pastry shells. Whenever it was my turn to pick berries, I swear I ate as many as I picked. The flavor was perfection.

At Windsor we gathered up loads of tender lettuces, sweet peas, dill, baby potatoes, and every kind of squash imaginable. The greenhouses yielded fragile tomatoes, potted Italian basil, and all sorts of herbs. With produce this good, half of a chef's work is already done. No wonder many chefs become absolutely besotted growers.

These days I get to garden year round. I don't have a large garden and ingenuity being the mother of invention, I've embraced aeroponic gardening.

During a family trip to Disney World I toured Epcot's Living With The Land, and the world's largest hydroponic showcase. As I rode through a supersize green house on a little boat I was amazed to see towers and towers of fruit and vegetables growing and all without soil.

I started researching hydroponic gardening and found a company that made tower gardens. These are vertical growing systems for the home that use aeroponics - an advanced form of hydroponics that grow plants in an air and mist environment using water and liquid nutrients but no soil. The solution is pumped to the top of the tower and then cascades down on to the roots of the fruit and vegetables. Using this vertical growing technique, I can boost the amount of food grown in my modest garden by a good deal. Best of all, between my tower garden and my regular beds, the view from my kitchen window in January is positively elysian.

I suspect I would be a gardener even if I wasn't a chef. The whole cycle, from seed to delicious fruit and vegetables, is a daily reminder of nature's timeless wonder and makes me grateful for every budding flower I see.

» *Supreme of Halibut Victoria, page 189*

IN GOOD COMPANY: A COZY DINNER FOR SIX

Growing up, while other kids got excited at the "pop man" turning into the street delivering bottles of dandelion and burdock, Irn Bru and cream soda, I always looked forward to Fridays when the fish man would deliver. You could smell the briny sea as soon as he opened his van back doors and I would peek in to see his supply of fresh fish. Living in the midlands most of our local fish was cod and haddock caught off Grimsby, a few miles north. My mum would go out to the van to buy fish for our usual Friday night fresh fish and chips. My dad would yell after her to "get me the tail end of cod with its head still on." It took me a few years to realize he was asking for a really large piece of fish for dinner! Fried in a delicious homemade batter with a plate full of homemade chips (fries) it was always a tea to look forward to.

These days, when I have my foodie friends over for a cozy dinner, I enjoy serving Supreme of halibut Victoria. It's a dish that we made in the Royal kitchens at Buckingham and is finished with a beautiful rich white wine cream sauce spooned over poached halibut, turbot or sea bass and garnished with lobster and delicate puff pastry fleurons. So old fashioned and so lovely. Halibut is available year round, but it is plentiful beginning in February and March. While they were once found in both the Atlantic and Pacific, these days the most sustainable halibut comes from Alaskan and Canadian Pacific waters. The sautéed beet greens and the accompanying salad round out the meal nicely.

CARA CARA ORANGE, CANDIED WALNUTS & STILTON CHEESE SALAD WITH BALSAMIC DRESSING

I LOOK FORWARD TO CARA CARA ORANGE SEASON. It's beautiful bright orange skin and almost raspberry colored sweet flesh makes an amazing winter salad. MAKES 4 PORTIONS

CANDIED WALNUTS

2 tablespoons unsalted butter

½ cup granulated sugar

1 pinch cayenne pepper

2 cups walnut halves

1 lightly greased baking sheet

BALSAMIC DRESSING

⅓ cup balsamic vinegar

1 cup olive oil

1 teaspoon Dijon mustard

1 teaspoon Cara Cara orange zest

Salt and pepper to taste

3 Cara Cara navel oranges, zested, peeled and segmented (set zest aside for dressing)

6 cups baby arugula/baby spinach mix

½ cup Stilton cheese, crumbled

2 tablespoons red onion, minced

¼ cup pomegranate seeds

1 **PREPARE THE NUTS** These can be made several days ahead and kept in an airtight container. In a heavy skillet add the butter, sugar cayenne and walnuts and cook on medium stirring until the butter has melted. Once the sugar starts to melt (about 5 minutes) stir the nuts more frequently so as not to burn them.

2 Once all the sugar has turned to syrup give one final stir and pour on to the greased baking sheet and spread out. Allow to cool completely before transferring to an airtight container. This recipe will make more than you need for the salad but they are great for snacking on too.

3 Zest the oranges and set aside for the salad dressing. Peel the oranges, segment and set aside.

4 Blend or whisk together the salad dressing ingredients and set aside. Any left over dressing will keep for a week in the refrigerator.

5 Place the salad leaves in a large bowl and top with the Stilton, red onion, oranges and pomegranate seeds. Drizzle a little of the dressing onto the salad and finish with the candied walnuts.

SUPREME OF HALIBUT VICTORIA

MAKES 4 PORTIONS

FISH BROTH
3 pounds fish bones, cleaned

3 stalks celery chopped

1 large leek, split and washed

2 onions, chopped

1 small fresh fennel bulb, chopped

3 garlic cloves, crushed

2 bay leaves

1 cup dry white wine

2 quarts water

4 (8 ounce) halibut fillets

2 lobster tails, lightly poached and sliced lengthways—shell off, dorsal vein removed

1 tablespoon unsalted butter

FOR THE SAUCE
1 cup heavy cream

1 cup champagne

¼ cup fresh chopped dill

Salt and pepper to season

1   Wash the fish bones in cold, clean water to remove impurities. In a large stock pot heat all fish broth ingredients to a boil. Cook over medium heat for 20 minutes and strain out and discard the vegetables and the bones.

2   Prep and set aside the lobster tails. Poach the halibut in the fish broth until just done (about eight minutes, or slightly longer depending upon the thickness of the halibut). Remove it from the poaching liquid and place it in a heatproof dish, cover and keep warm.

3   Reduce the fish broth by half over a high heat and add the cream and champagne. Reduce again to the consistency of pouring cream and adjust the seasoning. Sauté the lobster tails in butter to reheat, about two minutes each side and place on top of the halibut. Pour the sauce over the fish and lobster and garnish with the dill.

STIR-FRIED SHREDDED BEET & CHARD LEAVES

I REMEMBER MY GRANDAD COMING IN FROM HIS ALLOTMENT WITH BUNCHES OF PLUMP BEETS COVERED IN THICK SOIL. He would cut off the leaves, throw them away and wash the bulbs of beet (root) in the kitchen sink. I wish he was around today to show him how good those leaves are when washed, shredded and sautéed. Adding the chard balances the sweet beet leaves with a little bitterness creating a healthy vegetable dish. MAKES 4 PORTIONS

¼ cup olive oil

1 clove garlic, minced

8 cups chard leaves washed and shredded

8 cups fresh beet leaves washed and shredded

Salt and pepper to taste

¼ cup golden raisins

¼ cup pine nuts, lightly toasted

1 teaspoon apple cider vinegar

1 In a large skillet over medium heat add the oil and garlic and stir. Add the greens and a little salt and pepper and stir until they start to wilt but are still crunchy.

2 Stir in the raisins and apple cider vinegar, adjust the seasoning with salt and pepper and spoon into a serving dish. Garnish with the pine nuts.

BUTTERSCOTCH, STICKY PEAR PUDDINGS WITH CALVADOS CREAM

MAKES 4 RAMEKINS

BUTTERSCOTCH SAUCE
8 ounces unsalted butter (2 sticks)

½ cup honey

½ cup heavy cream

2 medium ripe pears

1 (125g) packet of Walkers Butterscotch Shortbread (or use the shortbread recipe from The Elegant Tea Menu and omit the lavender)

CALVADOS CREAM
1 cup heavy cream

2 teaspoons sugar

1 tablespoon Calvados

4 ramekins

1 Preheat the oven to 350°F.

2 In a large saucepan add the butter, honey and cream and place over high heat. Stir until it comes to a boil. Whisk for 3 minutes on high and pour about 1 tablespoon of the syrup into the bottom of each ramekin.

3 Peel, quarter and core the pears and slice into bite size pieces and arrange half of the pears into the ramekins. Roughly chop the shortbread into ¼ inch pieces and divide half of the mix between the ramekins over the pears and press firmly down.

4 Top the shortbread with the remaining pears and then another layer of shortbread and finish with a tablespoon each of the butter/honey/cream syrup poured on the four ramekins. Place the ramekins on a baking sheet and bake for about 20 minutes.

5 While the puddings are baking, whip the 1 cup of heavy cream and fold in the sugar and brandy.

6 When the puddings come out of the oven, allow to cool for at least 5 minutes before unmolding onto a plate. Top with the remaining butter, honey and cream syrup and serve with the Calvados cream.

» *Lobster Mac & Cheese Balls, page 194, and Turkey Meatballs with Smoked Paprika Coulis, page 196*

CELEBRATE THE SUPER BOWL

Full disclosure: I really don't know all that much about American football. I am, however, a committed "football" fan of another sort—soccer. Unfortunately that doesn't wash here in Texas. Grown men in white shorts kicking a ball does not, to most of my neighbors, a real sport make. No matter. I've decided to remain both a staunch year round (English) football fan and a once a year screaming lunatic when the Super bowl is on. But while British soccer food is simply a hot savory pie and cup of Bovril at half time, Super Bowl is a day devoted to armchair refereeing, drinking beer and inhaling calories like a defensive lineman. An almost perfect holiday!

The lineup (no pun intended) for the following menu is simple. To be appropriately competitive, there are mac and cheese balls with the addition of a bit of lobster. Then a fresh, citrusy ceviche that makes great use of all those tortilla chips on sale at the supermarket. Finally a meatball, that everyday ode to spherical perfection, simmered in a lovely, smoky paprika sauce that begs for a cold beer. Of course should the worst happen, I've also included a delicious chocolate bread pudding to lessen the bitter taste of defeat. Not to worry. There is always next year. Go Cowboys!

LOBSTER MAC & CHEESE BALLS

MAKES 12 BALLS

1 cup uncooked elbow macaroni

2 tablespoons butter

2 tablespoons flour

1 cup milk

¼ cup cream

Salt and pepper to taste

1 cup shredded mature English cheddar cheese

½ cup finely grated Parmesan cheese

1 cup chopped steamed lobster tail meat, or about two tails

Flour, eggs and panko breadcrumbs to coat balls

Vegetable oil for deep frying

1 In a medium saucepan, cook macaroni in boiling water until almost tender. Drain.

2 In a medium saucepan, melt the butter over medium heat. Stir in flour and cook for two minutes, stirring constantly. Whisk in the milk, cream salt and pepper. Bring to a bare simmer, then add the cheddar cheese and parmesan cheese and stir until melted. Remove from heat and stir in macaroni and lobster. Spoon mixture into deep dish and allow to cool.

3 Using an ice cream scoop shape the macaroni into small balls and roll in the flour followed by the beaten egg and finally the panko.

4 Heat oil in a deep frying pan or deep fryer to 350°F. Drop the mac and cheese balls into the oil and fry until golden. Sprinkle with salt and pepper and serve.

SALMON & CILANTRO CEVICHE WITH TORTILLA CHIPS

MAKES 10-12 CANAPES

8 ounces center cut fresh salmon steak, skinned and boned

Juice of 2 limes

¼ teaspoon salt

¼ teaspoon Huy Fong chili garlic paste

2 teaspoons sour cream

1 teaspoon capers

1 cup fresh cilantro, chopped

2 tablespoons extra virgin olive oil

Salt and sugar to taste

1 avocado

1 bag tortilla chips

1 Dice the salmon into ½ inch cubes. Mix it with the juice of the limes, salt and chili garlic paste. Cover and leave at room temperature for about 15 minutes stirring the fish delicately every now and then to allow it all to come into contact with the marinade. Once the fish has turned opaque, drain it and mix with the sour cream and capers.

2 Blend the cilantro with the oil and salt and sugar to a smooth sauce. Slice the avocado into small pieces. Lay out 10-12 tortilla chips and place a teaspoon of salmon on each one. Place a piece of avocado on top of the salmon and drizzle a little of the cilantro sauce over the top. Serve immediately.

TURKEY MEATBALLS
WITH SMOKED PAPRIKA COULIS

MAKES ABOUT 24 MEATBALLS

1 pound ground turkey

1 red bell pepper, finely diced

½ cup chopped fresh cilantro

½ cup chopped green onion

1 egg

⅓ cup panko or bread crumbs

1 teaspoon chili powder

½ onion, diced

2 tablespoons olive oil

2 tablespoons smoked paprika

2 cups heavy cream

Salt and pepper to taste

Toothpicks

1 Preheat the oven to 350°F. In a large bowl mix the turkey, pepper, cilantro, green onion, egg, panko, chili powder. Season with salt and pepper.

2 Shape the mix into small balls using an ice cream scoop and place on a greased baking sheet. Bake for about 10 minutes.

3 While the meatballs are cooking prepare the sauce. Sauté the onions in the olive oil until soft and translucent. Add the smoked paprika and stir. Add the cream and boil for about 4-5 minutes until reduced and thickened. Adjust the seasoning with salt and pepper.

4 Pour over the meatballs and serve.

WHISKY CHOCOLATE BREAD & BUTTER PUDDING

4 PORTIONS

3 chocolate croissants

¾ stick unsalted butter (6 ounces)

8 ounces semisweet chocolate

1 ½ cups sugar

¼ cup whisky (optional)

1 teaspoon instant espresso coffee

2 ½ cups heavy cream

2 egg yolks

3 eggs

1 (12x9x2) casserole dish

1 Preheat the oven to 350°F. Cut the chocolate croissants into two-inch cubes and place on the bottom of the casserole dish.

2 Place the butter and semisweet chocolate into a glass heat proof mixing bowl and microwave for about two minutes until they have both melted. Whisk in the sugar, whisky and coffee.

3 In a large mixing bowl whisk together the cream, egg yolks and whole eggs. Pour into the chocolate mix and whisk until combined.

4 Pour the egg and chocolate mix over the croissants and bake the casserole in the center of the oven for about 45 minutes. If the top of the pudding gets too brown loosely cover with aluminum foil. The center of the pudding should have a nice jiggle when shaken slightly, but not be too set. It will firm up as it cools down. Serve with ice cream or lots of whipped cream.

Tip: I will often slice bananas or fresh peeled and sliced pears on top of the croissants before pouring the chocolate egg mix on top.

VALENTINE'S DINNER FOR TWO

I n my perfect world, we would have more than one holiday a year devoted to celebrating love and I suspect we would be all the happier for it. I used to think that Valentine's Day meant an expensive dinner out with pricey wines and a big bunch of roses, but nowadays, I am relieved when my wife says, "let's stay in and you cook!"

I have to let you in on a secret… there are two days each year I hate to go out to restaurants: Mother's Day and Valentine's Day. Why? Well, everyone wants to eat out and restaurants try and turn over as many tables as possible. Attention to detail always suffers and I can't tell you how many times we have been disappointed with the food and service.

Valentine's day at home isn't hard to do. Prepare a menu you are comfortable with and do as much preparation as you can in advance. An easy salad with all of the ingredients pre-chopped in ziplock bags, ready to be tossed at the last minute. A simple steak with a few tiny roasted potatoes. Don't make anything too complicated, or too heavy. Keep the food simple and the wine flowing

This year I will again rattle pans in my own kitchen preparing Valentine's dinner for my wife, who is the glue that keeps our family together. I'll open a bottle of her favorite red wine, we'll chat in the kitchen and she will light the candles in the dining room to make the meal feel just a bit more special. We relax with meandering conversation leading neither here nor there and contemplate hazy future plans for the day when the nest is empty. The food always tastes great because for me, the magic ingredient is her company.

Happy Valentine's Day.

SPINACH & AVOCADO SALAD WITH WHOLE LEMON THYME DRESSING

THIS REALLY IS THE ZINGIEST SALAD DRESSING I MAKE. With "superfoods" like turmeric and honey in the dressing it's one of the healthiest too and goes with just about everything. This recipe also calls for sprouted walnuts which are walnuts that have been soaked in water overnight to reduce impurities and make them make easier to digest allowing all the nutritional benefits to be gleaned. Already soaked walnuts are available at Whole Foods, but I just make my own. Please note that I am using the whole lemon here—fruit, pith and rind—so do use an organic lemon that hasn't been sprayed. MAKES 4 PORTIONS

1 small organic lemon, cut into rough chunks

2 teaspoons Tupelo honey

½ cup cold pressed canola oil

1 teaspoon fresh, peeled turmeric

2 cloves garlic, finely minced

¼ cup fresh lemon juice

1 teaspoon salt

½ teaspoon black pepper

4 sprigs fresh thyme leaves

8 cups baby spinach leaves

4 avocados

½ cup sprouted walnuts

1 Place the whole lemon, honey, oil, turmeric, garlic, lemon juice and thyme leaves into the blender and pulse until smooth. Season with salt and pepper.

2 Cut the avocado into bite size pieces. Place the spinach leaves into a salad bowl and top with the avocado and walnuts. Drizzle some of the dressing over the salad leaves just before serving.

PAN SEARED BEEF TENDERLOIN STEAKS WITH A BURGUNDY CHOCOLATE SAUCE

RED WINE AND CHOCOLATE GO WELL TOGETHER, EVEN IN A SAUCE! This was one of my favorite sauces when I was cooking in the royal kitchens of Balmoral Castle. It goes incredibly well with venison tenderloin, but is just as delicious with beef too.

TIP: Use chocolate above 60% and add it right at the last minute. Don't boil the sauce once the chocolate has been added. Heat gently. MAKES 4 PORTIONS

4 (8 ounce each) center cut beef tenderloin steaks

2 tablespoons vegetable oil

BURGUNDY CHOCOLATE SAUCE

1 bottle Burgundy wine

2 cups chicken broth

1 onion cut in half

2 whole cloves

3 garlic cloves cut into halves

1 bay leaf

1 sprig of parsley

1 sprig of thyme

1 sprig of rosemary

2 carrots chopped

4 tablespoons softened unsalted butter

3 tablespoons flour

4 ounces dark chocolate

Salt and pepper to taste

1 MAKE THE SAUCE Combine the wine and broth in a big saucepan. Stick each onion half with a clove and add it to the pot along with the garlic, bay leaf, parsley, thyme, rosemary and carrots. Bring to the boil then reduce heat to medium and simmer until it is reduced to about half and the vegetables are very soft.

2 Strain this wine mixture pressing hard against the strainer to extract all the sauce and winey flavor. Discard the vegetables.

2 Return the sauce to the stove and heat through. Mix together the butter and flour then stir this in too letting it thicken and become glossy as it cooks. This should only take about 5 minutes. Break the chocolate into small pieces and whisk into the sauce. Season with salt pepper and keep warm

3 Preheat the oven to 400°F.

4 Season the steaks with salt and pepper. Heat a large skillet and add the vegetable oil. Sear the steaks until golden brown on all sides and place in the oven for about 6-8 minutes to required doneness. Remove the steaks from the oven and allow to rest for about 5-10 minutes. Spoon the sauce onto four plates and place a steak on top of the sauce.

SHORTBREAD LEMON PARFAIT

I USED TO PREPARE A LEMON PARFAIT AT BUCKINGHAM PALACE FOR VISITING KINGS, QUEENS AND PRESIDENTS. It was citrusy light but satisfyingly sweet. One of the joys of this recipe is that you can make it days ahead and leave it in the freezer until you sit down for dinner thus allowing more time with your loved one. SERVES 6 (2 PORTIONS ON VALENTINES DAY AND SOME IN THE FREEZER FOR WHEN FRIENDS COME OVER LATER IN THE WEEK)

Two (5.3 ounce) packs of Walkers pure butter shortbread fingers (or use the shortbread recipe from The Elegant Tea Menu and omit the lavender)

½ cup unsalted butter

½ cup granulated sugar + 2 tablespoons

3 lemons

5 egg yolks

½ pint heavy cream (at room temperature)

1 Place the two packs of Walkers pure butter shortbread fingers into a food processor and pulse until fine crumbs. Melt the unsalted butter and stir into the shortbread until combined. Spoon into heart shaped molds or a loaf tin and press down firmly. Refrigerate for about 30 minutes.

2 Zest the lemons and set aside. Juice the lemons and pass the juice through a fine sieve. Put the sugar, zest and juice in a pan and boil for about 3 minutes, until the sugar is melted and the mixture is slightly syrupy. Let cool.

3 In an electric mixer, whip the cream until it is stiff and set aside. With a clean bowl, whip the egg yolks until double the thickness, light in color and cold. Gradually pour in the lemon syrup mixture and whisk until combined. Fold in the cream and spoon into a 1 pound loaf tin, terrine or heart shaped molds.

4 Freeze overnight and unmold onto a plate or slice to serve with fresh berries and a little raspberry or chocolate sauce.

Note: Pasture eggs are best; they give a gorgeous rich yellow color to the finished dish

» *Darren's Beignets, page 209*

MARDI GRAS DANCE & DRINK

Mardi Gras (Fat Tuesday) is as much about partying as it is about the food, no matter where you are in the Christian world. In the UK, it's called Shrove Tuesday and every home cook is busy making pancakes, or crepes as the French call them. As fast as my mother would make them, my dad, brother, sister and I would sprinkle them with sugar and lemon juice and wolf them down. I continue the tradition today in my own household, though I am faster than my mum so I usually manage to eat one or two before the kids are yelling for more.

Shrove Tuesday is a long way from Mardi Gras, one of the American South's iconic holidays and one I've grown to love. I came to the States in 1997 and began working for a Texas family whose roots were in the South. My goodness, they loved Mardi Gras! At their urging, I learned how to make dishes that were less Texas and more bayou and from the start I was hooked on the spicy, layered flavors of Cajun/Creole cuisine. Not that there haven't been a few missteps. The first time I made grits I passed them through a sieve because they were too... well... gritty.

Still, I'm a quick learner and I've been told by many an effusive guest that I'm now pretty good at dishing up a traditional New Orleans Mardi Gras meal. While you may think that is just the Sazeracs and Hurricanes talking, I guarantee these recipes will have you reaching for your Mardi Gras beads and tossing your Zulu coconuts!

» Chili & Garlic Crusted Shrimp with Double Cheese Grits, page 207

CHILI & GARLIC CRUSTED SHRIMP WITH DOUBLE CHEESE GRITS

SERVES 4

FOR THE TRINITY
1 cup red bell peppers, cut into ½ inch dice

1 cup onions, cut into ½ inch dice

1 cup celery—cut into half inch dice

½ teaspoon dried thyme

1 clove garlic

2 tablespoons butter

FOR THE GRITS
3 cups water

1 cup quick grits

1 chicken bouillon cube

1 tablespoon butter

1 cup heavy cream

1 cup cheddar cheese, grated

1 cup parmesan cheese, grated

FOR THE SHRIMP
¼ cup butter

3 cloves garlic, crushed

2 pounds defrosted peeled and deveined Shrimp (21/25 count)

3 teaspoons chili powder

¼ cup chopped green onions

1   Prepare the trinity by sautéing the peppers, onions, celery thyme and garlic in the butter until softened. Remove to a small bowl and keep warm.

2   Prepare the grits. In a large heavy based pan bring the water to a boil and stir in the grits and broth cube. Whisk until the grits thicken and then add the butter and cream. Fold in the two cheeses and adjust the seasoning with sat and pepper. Cook for a further two minutes until the cheese melts and remove from the heat and cover.

3   Prepare the shrimp. In a large frying pan melt the butter and sauté the garlic. Add the shrimp and season with salt and pepper. Sear the shrimp on both sides and add the chili powder. Cook until tender—about 4 minutes and remove from the heat.

4   Spoon a generous portion of the grits onto each plate. Make a dent in the center of the grits with the spoon and place the shrimp in the middle. Spoon the trinity over the top of the shrimp and finish with the green onions sprinkled on top.

HEALTHY CHICKEN GUMBO

THIS DISH STARTS WITH A ROUX—A COMBINATION OF FLOUR AND OIL THAT COOKS UNTIL IT REACHES A CARAMEL COLOR. To make a good roux, do three things: Keep the heat moderate to ensure no scorching, take your time, and, most importantly, listen to Dr. John and the Medicine Show's classic recording of "Let the Good Times Roll." That should work. SERVES 4

¼ cup olive oil

⅓ cup flour

1 onion, peeled and chopped

1 red bell pepper, seeded and chopped

3 ribs celery, chopped

4 cloves garlic, minced

2 cups chicken broth

3 teaspoons Cajun seasoning

4 boneless, skinless chicken breasts, cut into bite size pieces

¼ cup green onions, chopped fine

1 In a heavy bottomed pan add the oil and flour over a medium heat stirring every few minutes. Once the flour and oil start turn color you will need to constantly stir. The "roux" needs to be a color between caramel and milk chocolate, so watch it closely and don't overcook. Once you have reached the perfect color quickly add the onion, pepper, celery and garlic and stir. Then stir in the chicken broth and Cajun seasoning followed by the chicken. Bring to a boil, stir, place a lid on top and reduce to a simmer and cook for about 30-40 minutes stirring occasionally.

2 Serve over brown rice or whole wheat pasta and sprinkle with the green onions to garnish.

DARREN'S BEIGNETS

THESE BEIGNETS HAVE A NICE SLOW OVERNIGHT RISE IN THE FRIDGE WHICH HELPS IMPROVE THEIR FLAVOR. That, and lots of powdered sugar! MAKES ABOUT 24

½ cup lukewarm water

4 cups bread flour

½ cup lukewarm milk

2 tablespoons butter, melted

1 large egg

¼ cup granulated sugar

2 teaspoons salt

2 teaspoons instant yeast

1 quart vegetable oil (for frying)

powdered sugar for decoration

1　In a large bowl mix all of the ingredients together to make a soft, smooth dough. Allow the dough to rise in a warm place, for about one hour. Flatten the dough, and place it into a greased bowl big enough to allow the dough to expand. Cover and refrigerate overnight.

2　Remove the dough from the refrigerator, and place it onto a lightly floured counter top. Roll the chilled dough into a rectangle about 1-inch thick. Cut the dough into 2-inch squares.

3　Heat the vegetable oil to 350°F, and place 6-8 of the dough pieces into the hot oil.

4　Fry the beignets for about two minutes, then turn them over to cook on the other side. Fry for another two minutes, until puffed and golden. Remove from the oil and drain on paper towels.

5　Sprinkle heavily with powdered sugar and serve.

» Beets with Papaya, Greek Yogurt, Pecans & Honey, page 212;
Guinness Braised Short Ribs, page 213;
and Kale and Goat Cheese Mashed Potatoes, page 214

A SUNDAY BRAISE WITH FRIENDS

This simple meal includes some of my favorite dishes, especially the fork tender braised beef short ribs. They are just what you want to eat during the cold winter months, especially paired with a kale and goat cheese mash which makes for a very comfort food combination.

Best of all the whole dinner can be assembled in advance. That's important for me when I have friends over. We all want to spend as much time as possible together, relaxing and having fun.

The ribs braise slowly in the oven and the kale and goat cheese mash can be made ahead of time and just re-warmed for dinner. All of the components of the salad can prepared ahead and put in ziplock bags and then assembled at the last minute, with a drizzle of dressing just before serving. Even the fallen soufflés are done and awaiting just a last minute touch.

BEETS WITH PAPAYA, GREEK YOGURT, PECANS & HONEY

ONE OF MY FAVORITE RESTAURANTS IN NEW YORK IS ABC KITCHEN. FRESH, ORGANIC AND LOCAL PRODUCE MAKE IT A "MUST VISIT" FOR ME EVERY TIME I AM IN THE BIG APPLE. They have a salad on the menu of roasted beets with homemade yogurt that is to die for. The first time I ate it I couldn't wait to get back to my kitchen to create my own twist on the dish. I love stirring the yogurt into the beets creating a purple cream that makes me feel like a child playing with food. MAKES 4 PORTIONS

2 large golden beets

2 large red beets

2 cups papaya peeled, seeds removed and cut into bite size pieces

1 cup Greek yogurt

4 cups baby arugula or spinach

1 tablespoon balsamic vinegar

2 tablespoons honey

¼ cup extra virgin olive oil

2 tablespoons roughly chopped dill

¼ cup chopped pecans (toasted)

1 teaspoon cumin seeds (toasted)

1 If you have a sous-vide machine cook the beets for one hour at 185°F. Cool, wipe off the skin with paper towel and cut into bite size pieces. Conventionally, place the beets in cold water (you must cook the red and gold beets in separate pans) Bring to the boil and simmer for about an hour or until the beets are tender when a knife is inserted. Cool the beets in cold water, remove the skin with paper towel and cut into bite size pieces.

2 In individual salad bowls spoon about ¼ cup of Greek yogurt. Arrange the beets and papaya pieces on top of the yogurt. Divide the arugula or spinach between the four salad bowls on top of the beets. Drizzle the vinegar, honey and olive oil on the leaves. Garnish with the dill, pecans and cumin seeds and serve.

GUINNESS BRAISED SHORT RIBS

4 PORTIONS

4 beef short ribs—bone in
(5 inches long, 2 inches thick)

Salt and pepper

3 tablespoons vegetable oil

6 strips smoked bacon

2 yellow onions, roughly chopped

3 carrots, roughly chopped

2 celery stalks, roughly chopped

6 garlic cloves, crushed

2 bay leaves

1 stick butter

½ cup flour

1 can Guinness

2 cups good strong beef broth
(or diluted "Better than Bouillon")

1 can diced tomatoes
(discard the juice)

1 Preheat an oven to 350°F.

2 Season the short ribs well with salt and pepper. In a large fry pan over medium-high heat add the oil and heat until almost smoking. Brown the ribs on all sides (about 3 to 5 minutes each side). Transfer to a Dutch oven or roasting pan.

3 In the same pan, now add the bacon and cook until it starts to crisp. Add the onions, carrots, celery, garlic, and bay leaves. Cook stirring occasionally, until all the vegetables star to soften, about 5 minutes. Season with salt and pepper. Spoon the vegetables over the ribs.

4 In the same pan, now melt the butter. Stir in the flour and incorporate with the butter. Add the Guinness and the broth. Bring to a boil. Add the diced tomatoes and season with salt and pepper. Pour the Guinness broth over the vegetables and ribs. Cover with a lid or aluminum foil and transfer your roasting pan to the oven. Bake until the meat is very tender, about 3-4 hours and the bones will push out of the meat.

5 Remove the meat to a serving dish. Skim the fat off the meat and then strain off and discard the vegetables. Taste the sauce for seasoning and pour over the meat.

6 Serve with mashed potatoes, kale and goat cheese mash, or soft polenta.

KALE & GOAT CHEESE MASHED POTATOES

MAKES 4 PORTIONS

2 pounds Yukon Gold potatoes, peeled and cut into large chunks

1 stick unsalted butter, divided

4 cloves garlic, minced

1 large bunch kale, stems discarded, shredded and rinsed thoroughly of grit

1 cup heavy cream

½ cup soft goat cheese, at room temperature

Salt and pepper, to taste

1 Place the potatoes in a large stockpot with and fill with water to cover. Salt well and bring to a boil. Cook potatoes for 15-20 minutes or until fork-tender.

2 Heat ½ stick of butter over medium heat in a large pan and saute the garlic and kale until tender, about 3-5 minutes, and set aside.

3 Drain the potatoes and return to pot. Mash with a potato masher and then add the cream gradually, mixing to incorporate. Season with salt and pepper to taste. Stir in the kale and then the goat cheese, adjust the seasoning and serve hot.

FALLEN CHOCOLATE SOUFFLÉS WITH AN AMARETTO CHOCOLATE BAVARIAN

WHEN YOU ARE GOING TO THE TROUBLE OF MAKING SUCH A DELICIOUS DESSERT AS THIS, IT REALLY IS WORTH MAKING A FEW EXTRA THAT YOU CAN REFRIGERATE AND ENJOY ALL OVER AGAIN LATER IN THE WEEK. MAKES 8 PORTIONS

FOR THE SOUFFLÉS

8 ounces dark chocolate

1 stick unsalted butter

4 eggs, separated

½ cup + ½ teaspoon sugar

1 teaspoon vanilla paste

1 cup pitted prunes, loosely packed

⅓ cup water

¼ cup port wine

FOR THE BAVARIAN

6 ounces dark chocolate

1 teaspoon vanilla paste

10 fluid ounces heavy cream, whipped to soft peak

5 egg yolks

1 teaspoon instant coffee, dissolved in 2 teaspoons hot water

2 tablespoons Amaretto

1 jar clotted cream or whipped heavy cream

1 container of blackberries to garnish

1 The day before you make the soufflés, take the prunes and simmer for 5 minutes in ⅓ cup boiling water. Remove them from the heat and add the port wine. Refrigerate overnight.

2 Preheat the oven to 350°F. Line 8 four ounce ramekins with softened butter and sugar.

3 Melt the chocolate and the butter until combined and stir in the prunes and syrup

4 Beat the egg yolks and the sugar until pale and fluffy and add to the chocolate mix. Whip the whites until stiff and fold into the chocolate mix. Spoon into the prepared soufflé dishes and bake for about 15 minutes. Remove from the oven and invert onto a lightly buttered tray to cool.

5 Prepare the Bavarian. Melt the chocolate and whisk in the egg yolks, vanilla paste, Amaretto and coffee. Fold in the whipped cream and refrigerate until it starts to set. Spoon over the top of the chilled soufflés, garnish with the cream and blackberries and serve.

NOTES ON ENTERTAINING

*"For you know that alone
we cannot share life. Others must be there."*

– Diego Vasquez Pacheco –

Both professionally and personally, I've thrown what feels like a million parties in my life. From lavish state banquets served off of three hundred year old Meissen china in the Buckingham Palace ballroom, to hand packed Tupperware meals for picnics in the Balmoral countryside, to expansive barbeques on vast Texas' ranches and chatty cocktails parties at sea, I've had a hand in lots and lots of get togethers. Amazingly, I still look forward to the next one! From years of observation, I've cobbled together some very general guidelines about what seems to make dinner parties go smoothly, for host and guest. I think of them in four categories: comfort, style, organization and menu.

COMFORT

Comfort is at the very heart of hospitality. While there are those rare people who seem utterly at home no matter the situation, they are the exception rather than the rule. I am lucky to have two friends whose names go on my list first for every party. They meticulously and naturally work their way around the room introducing, connecting and networking; it makes my job as host a lot easier. Recognizing early on how to make your guests comfortable goes a long way to creating a relaxed evening. So here are a couple of tips:

• A friendly hello and a freshly made drink is a must. Welcoming guest into your home and introducing them around is a basic kindness and helps to get the conversation going. If it's a familiar group of friends, then you don't have to do much. On the other hand, if the guests are strangers to one another, take a moment for introductions and help them make connections. Kids at the same school? Same college? Eaten at any good restaurants lately? Find the common ground, "So, are the girls going to win our important soccer game on Saturday then?" before slipping gently into the background to top up drinks and let the conversation build. By all means, feel free to invite new guests into the kitchen and give them a job. Everyone feels more relaxed washing lettuce than finding new topics to discuss. Plus helping with the meal creates a sense of intimacy, even among strangers. Soon your eclectic gathering will be off down interesting conversational paths toward (hopefully) new friendships.

- Have sufficient lighting and seating. Avoid the extremes; make sure the room isn't too dark or too bright. I've been to dinner parties where all the lighting in the home was provided via little tea lights. That can be fine if you use lots and lots and lots of tea lights. If not, you are essentially eating in the dark. Informal seating arrangements work fine as long as they include a few comfortable chairs and table nearby to put down a drink or a plate. Don't feel you have to have a chair for everyone though. You want guests to circulate and get a chance to move around the room. Just give people some options.
- Try to be present. Don't separate yourself overlong from your guests. Sure, there is always some last minute work to do in the kitchen, but build a menu that let's you enjoy the party too.
- Don't spring surprises on your guests. Let them know exactly what type of event they are invited to. Is it formal or casual? Does it have a firm end time? Does it involve a costume? That last one is important! It's a

silly British tradition to wear paper crowns at Christmas supper and some of my Texan friends have made it clear in no uncertain terms ("Are you kidding? Hell no") that the paper crown is not exactly their cup of tea. If it makes them uncomfortable, then off with the crown!

STYLE

Personal style is something we all have even if some of us are convinced our style button is on mute. My anecdotal experience tells me that stylewise, people generally fall into two camps; the minimalists and the maximalists. The minimalist loves a perfect single flower in a beautiful vase, the green of asparagus spears set off against a large white plate and room décor which is cool, uncluttered and open. The maximalist, on the other hand, loves big bouquets of flowers, rooms filled with personal mementos and platters of food filled to the brim. Im hard pressed to prefer one over the other, for in fact, I like them both.

Whatever your style, it should be expressed in appropriate measure to the event. For example, some of us just love the look of a white linen tablecloth, shining crystal and silver and individually plated dinners. Lovely. But certainly not practical for an event with forty guests! So, the linen stays, the silver and napkins can be rolled up and tied, the individual plates set off to the side and bring out the elegant platters filled with food.

Spend a minute and think about what you find beautiful in your home. You may have wonderful pearl colored shells picked up on your last trip to the beach and wouldn't that look nice with candles tucked in around it as a centerpiece. What about your collection of brightly colored mid-century pottery and a big bouquet of sunflowers? Without being aware of it, you've already got what you need. Just take a closer look, be creative and go ahead and make a splash.

ORGANIZATION

Doing things in advance always makes entertaining more enjoyable for the host. With all the big jobs out of the way you can relax and enjoy the flow of conversation. Plus planning saves you time, money and aggravation. Take quick stock of your budget, your pantry and liquor cupboard and decide what kind of party would be best. Since most gatherings will be "host powered" you should be realistic about what you can do and what shortcuts will work. Some dishes you may make yourself, but if one of your guests asks what he/she can bring and you know them to be handy in the kitchen, well then graciously say 'absolutely'! Being a chef, I usually plan the menu in advance. But if I know someone who loves to cook, I might pick up the phone and cajole my guest with "Actually, I love that shrimp appetizer that you made last time you had us over. I don't suppose you fancy rustling that up for us do you?" Trust me, the guest will put down the phone, pleased at the compliment.

I like to get as much of the food preparation done ahead of time as possible. Ill marinate meat, wash and prep salads, make vinaigrettes, cut up veggies which only need a quick roast or steam and have desserts chilled and ready to pull out when needed. When I have certain wine connoissuers friends come to dinner, I always serve a cold dessert ready to pull out of the refrigerator at a moments notice. Forget whipping egg whites and folding into soufflé

mix in the kitchen, when a decanter of Pauillac is being emptied around the dining table too fast for my liking!

I also always set up my bar tray in advance and get the table or sideboard ready. Then I know I won't be endlessly in the kitchen while all the fun is happening on the other side of the door. My experiences as a chef and my pleasure as an invited guest are reflected in the menus I've put together, so that you can be both a great cook and fabulous host.

For big events, and they do come up from time to time, consider party rentals. Trust me, china plates that can be stacked in the garage at the end of the evening for someone else to wash is a huge help. There is a time and place for a caterer too—one who is highly recommended by friends and whom you feel is flexible and responsive to your needs. Good caterers bring along their staff and it's great to know that someone else will be cleaning up the kitchen at the end of the night.

Remember, the more you entertain the better you get at it. One friend of mine has recently jettisoned all appetizers during the summer. After all, she reasoned, it's just too hot and appetites aren't robust. So, she sets out a pitcher of cold cocktails, iced gin and tonics or perhaps an "in vogue" mixed drink like a Pimms Cup and lemonade for everyone. It cools people down, gets conversation flowing and primes appetites for dinner. Best of all... it's easy.

MENU

Well now to the heart of the matter: What's to eat? I hope the menus I've assembled in this book entice you into the kitchen to recreate or to give your own special twist. But a few quick pointers before we start.

Keep it simple. Now is not the time to pull out the recipe torn from last Wednesday's food section to prepare for the boss coming to dinner—just because it looks good in the photo. Test drive that dish for when it's just the family. If it's a mess, who cares... where's the bread, peanut butter and jelly? I want this book to be the one you pull out of the draw each time you say "let's have a party" because you know that each and every recipe works and wows, and because they are easy and familiar.

Keep the food on the recognizable side and be sensitive to guest preferences. You want your guests to have tried Thai squid salad a few times at their favorite Thai restaurant before you spring on them as a main course. Tweak an old favorite instead. How about some shrimp sates with peanut sauce and a regular green salad. Most people can handle that easily. A word of host liberation though; you are by no means required to kowtow to guests who have endless dietary, health, or emotional issues with food. Invite those friends to a movie or a trip the museum, not to dinner. If you can, and I realize that isn't always possible, try to invite people who can eat without bouts of excessive anxiety. Enjoyment and relaxation, yours included, are the keys to a great evening.

Match the menu to the event. A barbeque should have a nice casual feel to it from the menu choices to the setting. You may decide to favor lamb over hot dogs and that's great. Just keep the menu easy, low key and in the spirit of outdoor cooking. Along with that lamb, you can have grilled flatbreads, chunks of grilled peppers and onions, yogurt tzatziki and a classic greek salad. Perfect hot weather food. Or maybe some large shrimp tossed in olive oil, garlic and chili to sear on the grill. Toss a drained can of cannellini beans into the food processor with some fresh garlic, lemon zest and juice, olive oil and salt and pepper. Spoon into the center of a large bowl, place the shrimp on top and serve with some crisp pita chips.

Easy, craft menus which have some dishes you can do ahead of time combined with those that require your attention at the last minute, is simply a more practical approach and it also yields some nice contrasts between food served at room temperature and hot dishes ready to go.

Don't forget to taste. Even after I have made the same recipe for years and years, I still taste as I go along. I find this is one of the fundamental differences between a chef and a home cook. Take mashed potatoes for example. How many people go to the trouble of peeling potatoes, waiting for them to cook and then mashing the lumps out of them only to sprinkle in a bit of salt, stir and serve them. The chef will season, taste, season again—more cream, a little butter, two grates of nutmeg, sprinkle of kosher salt and freshly ground pepper. Sometimes I've forgotten an ingredient or I've made an ill-advised substitution or I know that my guests like things more mildly or strongly spiced. By tasting as I go along, I give myself a chance to make mid-course corrections. That saves me a lot of time and money. I wish I had listened to my own advice the night I cooked dinner for Prince Andrew when he was dating

Sarah Ferguson. If I had, I would surely have known that the pastry I was rolling out for his salmon quiche was in fact the sugar pastry I had made earlier for the Queen's apple pie the next day!

Respect the bounty of the seasons. Ripe strawberries define the warmth of late spring just as a roasted turkey is an autumn rite of passage. Eating seasonally provides opportunities to try new ingredients and expand our cooking repertoire. Besides, eating in season means better tasting ingredients and better flavor means your job is half done for you. No matter what our clever agricultural scientists try to do, a strawberry in winter still tastes like a cottony apple. Yuck. Plus there is cost to consider. Peach bellinis are a lot less expensive to make in June than in January. Seasonal menus are in vogue right now and I think that's a great thing. We should eat what is fresh, in season, grown locally and is of good value. It fixes our celebrations in place and time making them even more memorable.

One final note. Don't worry if the meal doesn't turn out exactly as expected. The food is there to complement the evening, not define it. Pour yourself a nice drink, settle in with your guests, catch up on all the gossip and have fun.

INDEX